Love, Norm

Inspiration of a Jewish American Fighter Pilot

Norman M. Shulman

TEXAS TECH UNIVERSITY PRESS

This book is typeset in EB garamond. The paper used in this book meets the minimum requirements of ANSI/NISO Z39.48-1992 (R1997). ♾

Designed by Hannah Gaskamp

Unless otherwise noted, all photographs are from the collection of the author.

Library of Congress Cataloging-in-Publication Data

Names: Shulman, Norman M., 1947– author. Title: Love, Norm: Inspiration of a Jewish American Fighter Pilot / Norman M. Shulman. Other titles: Inspiration of a Jewish American fighter pilot Description: Lubbock, Texas: Texas Tech University Press, [2022] | Series: Modern Jewish history | Includes bibliographical references and index. | Summary: "An epistolary memoir, featuring letters from the author to his stepson in the Air Force along with profiles of historical Jewish military heroes, ruminating on Jewish identity, heroism, history, and inspiration"—Provided by publisher. Identifiers: LCCN 2021038558 (print) | LCCN 2021038559 (ebook) | ISBN 978-1-68283-124-3 (paperback) | ISBN 978-1-68283-131-1 (ebook)
ISBN 978-1-68283-168-7 (hardcover)
Subjects: LCSH: Shulman, Norman M., 1947– | Jewish soldiers—Biography. | Jews—United States—Identity. | Levenson, Greg, 1978—Family. | Fighter pilots—United States—Correspondence. | Psychologists—United States—Biography. | Jews—Texas—Lubbock—Biography. Classification: LCC E184.37 .S535 2022 (print) | LCC E184.37 (ebook) | DDC 358.40092 [B]—dc23
LC record available at https://lccn.loc.gov/2021038558
LC ebook record available at https://lccn.loc.gov/2021038559

Printed in the United States of America
22 23 24 25 26 27 28 29 30 / 9 8 7 6 5 4 3 2 1

Texas Tech University Press
Box 41037
Lubbock, Texas 79409-1037 USA
800.832.4042
ttup@ttu.edu
www.ttupress.org

Dedicated to Maj. Gen. Stanley Newman

Nixon: "I didn't notice many Jewish names coming back from Vietnam . . ."

Colson: "Well they don't go out and fly airplanes, that's one thing."

Nixon: "They sure as hell aren't in the Air Force."

—From the White House tapes of President Richard M. Nixon to Chuck Colson, Director of the Office of Public Liaison, February 1973

"Who said Jews can't fight?"

—General Stan Newman

Contents

Illustrations

Acknowledgments

DAYENU, THE HEBREW WORD FOR "ENOUGH," IS the name of a much-beloved Passover song that extols God's many gifts to the Jews during the exodus. It goes something like this: If God had only freed us from Egyptian bondage, *dayenu*; if God had only bestowed us the Torah, *dayenu*; if God had only sustained us during the Sinai wandering, *dayenu*; and if God had only delivered us to freedom in the promised land, it would have been enough. *Dayenu*.

The song reminds me of the timely, consistent, and essential support I received from the team that stood with me during the long development of this book. First and foremost, I am extremely and forever grateful to my TTU Press editors, Joanna Conrad and Travis Snyder, who were confident that I could transform my narrative into a memoir. Special thanks to Christie Perlmutter, who practiced copyediting to perfection. Much appreciation also goes to Hannah Gaskamp, senior designer, and to Kate Despres, who assisted with the index and other aspects of the book's preparation. I thank Suzanne Vincent Bonds for providing counsel during this process, researching many of the historical figures and skillfully editing the many ensuing drafts.

Great thanks go to my sisters. To Linda, for telling me repeatedly through the years that I always had a book in me. To Fifi, for nurturing my early interest in reading and never allowing me to be neglected. I am thankful to Byron Price, who initially greenlighted the idea and encouraged me to complete it while "hangin' and rattlin'" all along the way. And to my loving wife, Carol, who balanced being my most astute and vocal critic and my greatest fan at the same time. I love you with all my heart.

Last but not least, I thank Greg Levenson and all his unnamed yet inspirational precursors who constitute the foundation of this story. They offer demonstrable, incontrovertible evidence that not only did Jews answer the call, they fought like hell with the best of them. *Dayenu.*

Love,
Norm

Introduction

"Jews are different; their history makes them different."

—Jewish saying

I WAS NOT SHOCKED WHEN MY STEPSON DECIDED to become a fighter pilot. As a child, Greg Levenson possessed exceptional hand–eye coordination honed during many hours of video gaming as well as a keen interest in and fascination with flight and the military. I can't count the number of air shows we went to. Attending space camp was a no-brainer. Even when he earned a pilot's license and began flying frequently at seventeen, though, he expressed no interest in pursuing a career in the military. Most people who knew him figured flying was just a hobby, something he would outgrow. But he only became more passionate about flight and serving his country.

Once I embraced Greg's dream, I rarely missed an opportunity to connect him to anyone who might spur him on toward his quest. So, upon hearing that a colleague would be stopping in Lubbock during a cross-country training mission in an F-16, I asked if it would be appropriate to meet him and show Greg his Viper jet.

After our brief visit at the airport, the pilot requested and received permission to do a high-performance takeoff. If you haven't seen one, it is truly awe inspiring. The jet comes barreling down the runway and then dramatically accelerates into a vertical ascension. I'll never forget the look on Greg's face at that moment. It said, "Damn, I want to do that!" (At Greg's "Fini Flight," or his last time in the F-16, on September 28, 2010, he performed the same maneuver.)

While it has always been important to me to support Greg in any way that would help him fulfill his potential, I also had a deeply personal reason for him to attain his goal. While arranging for the publication of an article titled "My Son, the Fighter Pilot," which I wrote for *The Jewish Veteran* in 2008, I had a timely conversation with one of the magazine's administrative personnel. She informed me that just after the submission of my article, she received a phone call from an eleven-year-old boy, presumably Jewish, who asked if there were any Jewish fighter pilots. This simple question, one that a Christian boy would not have had to ask, reflects the innocent ignorance that has perpetuated a lingering Jewish stereotype.

It would be safe to assume that this curious young man may have been stirred by the prospect of flying fighter jets. However, not yet possessing sufficient knowledge of his people's history brought him to ask such a question. His experience is an unfortunate extension of the general impression of Jews as nonwarriors at best and shirkers of their military responsibilities at worst. While far less prejudice exists in the present day it still persists, and this book was written against the backdrop of this misperception.

When I was eleven, I had my initial exposure to the idea that Jews are somehow less courageous than their Christian counterparts. In the movie *Gentleman's Agreement* (1947), a journalist, played by Gregory Peck, passes himself off as a Jew to do a story on anti-Semitism. A scene occurs in a nightclub where another soldier assumes from his name (Green) that Peck served in a noncombatant role during World War II. Peck angrily repudiates the crass insult, and I remember even as a child getting great satisfaction from this comeuppance.

After all, I had three maternal uncles who served their country admirably during World War II, one of whom earned the Bronze Star for courage under fire. As a result, the denigrating assumption made in the movie was both puzzling and infuriating. At that time I was totally unaware of the myth that had affected attitudes toward Jews regarding their relative lack of participation in the military. I simply took it for granted that Jews were appreciated for the scope of their sacrifices just like any other ethnic group that served with distinction in America's wars.

After graduating from the University of Texas and flying a desk at a bank for five years, Greg realized that his window of opportunity to fulfill a childhood dream was rapidly closing. The cutoff age of twenty-seven was nearly upon him, so in 2005 he applied for and was accepted into a pilot training position with the New Mexico Air National Guard, and he took a leave of absence from his job.

The family's initial response was lukewarm at best. Many of them were ambivalent about the military as far as a career was concerned. They wondered how Greg could give up so much to do something so dangerous rather than pursue a conventional career.

In April 2005, he began the arduous physical, emotional, and intellectual hurdles that were part of the requisite thirteen months of Undergraduate Pilot Training (UPT) at Vance Air Force Base in Enid, Oklahoma. It was there that he first experienced spiritual isolation. At the time he was under the impression that he was the only one of Jewish faith on the entire base of over nine hundred airmen. (We later found out that one other Jewish pilot, a colonel, was also stationed at Vance.) That paucity, coupled with some anti-Semitic comments, were harsh realities that accentuated his isolation. His resolve to retain his Jewishness was immediately tested by his relative uniqueness in the world of military pilots.

I became aware of Greg's spiritual isolation during a telephone conversation I had with him early in his training. My protective parental instincts kicked in, and I began to think of ways to affirm his spiritual identity during this difficult time.

After a few more conversations and knowing that training would be hard enough without having to deal with people who did not like him just because of what he is and what he believes, I set about on my

Author and stepson Greg Levenson. (Photo credit Carol Levenson)

own journey into Jewish military history to show him that he was following a well-worn tradition. This exploration initiated the series of letters that I began writing to encourage him with examples showing that he was far from alone. During his next year of flight training, I wrote fifty-two letters about a multitude of Jewish war heroes. Greg said that sometimes he would save them and read them all at once when he had enough time to appreciate the stories. At other times, he would read them immediately if he needed inspiration after a particularly hard day or before a challenging task. That was gratifying for me to hear. Greg is not a complainer. I knew that if he was distressed it had to be serious. Knowing that he'd had a tough day and needed a push from my letters told me that, as for all who seek extremely demanding professions, support meant everything.

Along with discovering unforgettable Jewish figures from military history, I delved into the military histories of our families and friends. I was determined to keep the stories flowing in order to inspire Greg to attain his dream.

The Jewish Military Hero of the Week was attached at the end of each letter. These individuals' use of their faith helped them cope with their ordeals of war and anti-Semitism, often at the same time. They never renounced their Judaism nor blamed it for their struggles. Rather, their understated endurance was inspirational.

In retrospect, Greg and I had very different but historically connected responses to his minority status. He wondered why he had no other Jewish peers in the military. Where were his family members and many Jewish friends and acquaintances whom he had made during his lifetime? I, on the other hand, thought of his isolation in terms of historical prejudice. In truth, negative experiences in Jews' countries of origin have affected their collective consciousness regarding attitudes toward the military. With a few notable exceptions in countries that allowed Jews to advance in the armed services, Jewish parents were fearful for their children's security and therefore emphasized education—particularly the professions as a means of elevating themselves in society. Since Judaism has always made education a high priority, this generational transition of values took and maintained a fast hold.

The reader may question the overall importance of this subject matter. After all, in the greater scheme of things, anti-Semitism in the military as described here—other than a few extreme examples (see Tibor Rubin)—could easily be seen as a mere inconvenience of the Jewish experience. However, of the many elements of historical anti-Semitism, I argue that a perceived lack of patriotism is the most destructive. This stereotype, which Greg was going to fly against (so to speak), has been successfully used as part of an anti-Semitic narrative by those bent on the discrimination, persecution, national expulsion, and in more recent times the annihilation of the Jewish people.

Unfortunately, this false impression of Jewish military service has appeared in many countries throughout history. For example, an Australian Jewish soldier, Jake Kleinman, noted that even among Jews there was puzzlement at the idea that a Jew might be a foot soldier. He spoke to Jews who couldn't believe that a Jew would voluntarily join an army other than the Israeli army but that one would be expected to be a doctor or a lawyer or something other than an infantryman.

None other than Mark Twain reinforced this misperception by once writing, "The Jew is charged with a disinclination patriotically to stand by the flag as a soldier." While Twain retracted this statement years later, his earlier writings reveal this widely circulated prejudice.

A famous nineteenth-century historian, Cornell professor Goldwin Smith, posited that Jewish tribalism and an unwillingness to declare loyalty to a particular country prevented them from being patriotic. As a result, it is essential that the perception of Jewish cowardice in the context of national loyalty be consistently resisted. History has provided all the objective proof that is required to set the record straight. In response to allegations that no Jews served during the Civil War, in 1895 Simon Wolf published the names and states of origin of over eight thousand Jews who served on both sides. More recently, similar documentation listing Jews who served in the Spanish–American War and in the Australian and New Zealand armed forces dating back to the nineteenth century was established.

As Mark Dapin described in *Jewish Anzacs*, Col. Kerrie Davies served so heroically for his queen and country that he was recommended for the Victoria Cross (VC) by his commanding officer. The VC is the British equivalent of the Medal of Honor. However, true to his word upon entering the military that he expected no reward for his services under any circumstance, he declined the medal. According to Col. Davies, he performed as he was supposed to and therefore

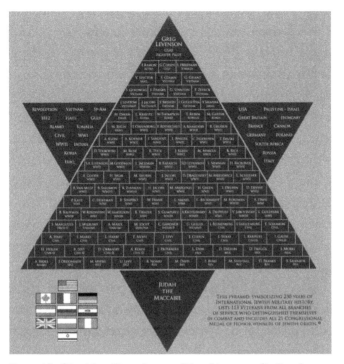

Pyramid of Jewish military heroes. (Graphic art credit Carol
Levenson)

considered his extraordinary bravery as nothing special. It goes without saying that historians would be hard pressed to find similar examples of such humility and patriotic reverence. As a result, I saw the
material in this book first as an opportunity to help strengthen Greg's
identity but now also to add to the literature against a pernicious
stereotype. During this process I discovered an incredible array of
Jewish military figures who played key roles during critical times in
American and world history.

Jewish distinction in military history begins with Judah the Maccabee
(*maccabee* is "hammer" in Hebrew) at the base. Judah is acknowledged
to be the greatest of Jewish warriors; his exploits led to the rededication
of the Temple after it had been desecrated by the Assyrian Greeks in
Roman times (170 BCE). The holiday of Hanukkah or "dedication" is
a commemoration of this momentous military victory.

The flags to the bottom left of the pyramid represent all the countries for which this book's Jewish heroes fought. Greg's name is the 113th of the veterans listed, and it rests at the top of the pyramid supported by all the other Jewish warriors who paved the way for him by setting inspirational examples.

Most of the names on the pyramid have been plucked from historical obscurity and represent the international participation of the Jew at war. The Talmud instructs that Jews are obligated to fight for their country, and they did—wherever the Diaspora left them. Most of the names in the figure represent people who distinguished themselves as combatants. They include all seventeen Medal of Honor winners of Jewish origin and highly decorated Jewish soldiers and airmen from other countries.

As for the criteria for inclusion on the pyramid and in the letters, the definition of "hero" was somewhat nonspecific. For the most part it applied to distinguished Jewish combat veterans honored for their service. However, occasionally I included others who by their very identity as a Jew encountered daunting challenges their Gentile peers didn't have to face. In addition, a few characters were added due to their behind-the-scenes contributions to significant historical events.

Because of Greg's desire to become a fighter pilot, I weighted the list with airmen, two of whom he knew: his grandfather Sam Levenson and a family friend, Bernie Barasch. The exploits of both in mortal combat, which are briefly described later, greatly inspired Greg as a young boy. The pyramid lists several Jewish pilots who flew with the Royal Air Force in the most significant air battle in history, the Battle of Britain, and includes the unquestionably greatest Jewish fighter pilot of all time, Flt. Lt. Robert Stanford Tuck, who recorded thirty air victories against the Nazis.

CHAPTER 1

God Laughs

"Man plans and God laughs."

—Jewish proverb

GREG LEVENSON AND I FIRST MET ON A CRUISE ship on March 15, 1986. We bonded quickly in spite of the fact that his parents were in the process of a divorce. Most children struggle at these times trying to develop healthy relationships with their parents' new friends. Greg didn't. From the onset he was capable of balancing his father and me with little or no internal conflict or behavioral problems.

In Greg's mind his dad and I had our set roles, and Greg was able to integrate each of us into his life. Even on the rare occasions that his father and I were placed together by circumstance, he never flinched or was uncomfortable or conflicted. This remains true to the present day.

Many years later, I recognized that this quality was an essential strength. A combat fighter pilot's ability to calmly compartmentalize difficult simultaneous situations could be the difference between life and death. As a child, Greg spared me from feeling compromised by my entrance into his world. As an adult he spared me from unnecessarily worrying that he would be dangerously distracted by any competing challenges he would have to confront.

Having no military training, and certainly no flight experience other than being a passenger, I offered Greg what I did have to help advise him on his path, and that's being the son of immigrant Jews, with many experiences of isolation. My father, Mike, immigrated to the United States from Bialystok, Poland, at the age of eleven or so. Although he was assigned the birth date of August 1, 1898, upon arrival at Ellis Island, due to a brutal draft system in czarist Russia and pervasive anti-Semitism, Jewish parents protectively masked their boys' ages by not recording their birth dates. Pop made the voyage with his father aboard the SS *Zeeland* in steerage (fifth class), subsisting on crackers for the two-week trip. My father clearly remembered clambering on deck among all the other passengers to see the Statue of Liberty when they steamed into New York Harbor.

Upon arrival my father, born Meyer Yosef Szczerb, became Martin Joseph Shulman, but everyone knew him as Mike. Later we found out that his birth year may have actually been 1896 and that he had his Bar Mitzvah (at thirteen) in America, which provides some temporal context.

Mike always had problems with authority, likely stemming from years of living under czarist Russian oppression, where anti-Semitism was rampant. He was also the product of a very strict upbringing. The Jewish community in his hometown was so isolated that he spoke only Yiddish while growing up.

In September 1918, near the end of World War I, Pop was drafted into the New Jersey Shore Artillery. The family has exactly one picture of him at that age, the only picture of him before his marriage to my mother. Within two months, he was busted in rank from private first class to buck private. When asked what happened, he wryly replied, "I didn't like being told what to do."

Pop never finished formal school and went to work in order to help his large family. He had a series of odd jobs, mostly in some form of retail, until he met his eventual partner with whom he went into the "entertainment business." Mike was a colorful Runyonesque character who recognized that there were quicker but nontraditional ways to make money.

Pop and his partner established a front, called the Victory Club, for a gambling operation in the 1930s in Syracuse, New York. He and Louie would supply the liquor, food, and cover to operate what amounted to banned card games. In one year Mike and his partner split over one hundred thousand dollars, an enormous sum during the Depression. I remember being awestruck at his success. I then asked why he held his interest in the Victory Club for only one year. He soberly replied, "Because I didn't want to go to jail." Lesson learned.

Shortly thereafter, my parents met. My mother's name was Bertha Margolis. My father hired her to run a cash register in a store he was managing. My mother promptly toppled the register onto his foot. It must have been love at first wince, for they married soon after.

Mike was about thirty-five and my mother was eighteen when they wed. At that time the age difference was acceptable to her parents because, relatively speaking, he was an established businessman. (I doubt they knew about the Victory Club.) Both of her parents were refugees from Kiev, Ukraine, and saw the arrangement as a means of ensuring her future security.

A year after they married, my sister Linda was born in 1934. The Shulmans settled into life, opting to affiliate with a Conservative Jewish synagogue to which my father belonged—and where they stayed until 1981, when they were forced to relocate to Miami after my mother had a stroke. As with many other Jewish immigrant families, they started out keeping kosher but gradually gave in to convenience and became less observant. They did draw a line and did not assimilate completely. Their identities as Jews bent but never wavered in spite of my father's business and my mother's strong ecumenical charitable interests.

Pop next went into the nightclub business, where he thrived. The Club Miami was the professional highlight of his life. It offered a complete gamut of entertainment, including a band, singers, dancing, and yes, drag performers, a big draw back then. The featured act was the Lyle Page Boys Will Be Girls Review. I have the newspaper advertisement to prove this.

Mike's engaging personality, warmth, openness, humor, inclusiveness, and listening ability were all conducive to his success. He was most comfortable in his bowtie and crisp white shirt, greeting customers and being behind the bar. People could have drunk the same alcohol anywhere, but they came to schmooze with Mike Miami.

Later in life when well into my career as a psychologist he asked me how I decided to become one. He was dead set on my becoming a "real doctor" and couldn't understand how I could ever make a living by listening and talking to people. I couldn't help but laugh and point to the qualities we shared, which indicated that I was born to do what I do and that his influence was instrumental in my decision. Mike was taken aback by the irony but couldn't deny it—although he never quite gave up the "real doctor" ideal.

My sister Phyllis, or Fifi as almost everyone called her, was born in 1939. I was last, born in 1947. Due to the relative closeness in age between us, I spent much more time with her growing up and beyond than with Linda. Fifi was a great sister in that she included me in many of her high school and college activities. I spent a lot of time in the backseat of cars while she was on dates. I never felt left out or wanting for something to do.

For the first seven years of my life, until 1955, our family of five lived in a three-bedroom walkup flat along with two of my mother's brothers, Leon and Irv (Odie) Margolis. The uncles were included to give them a leg up toward work. No one thought twice about all of us sharing one bathroom or limited living space. It was just something that families did.

Growing up being Jewish was something I took for granted until I was about six, when an elementary school experience changed everything. I attended Brighton Elementary for almost three years, with only one other Jewish classmate, Carl Wolkin. How did I know this?

Tuesday afternoon was religious instruction day. At about 2 p.m. or so, all the Catholic students went to a nearby church while all the Protestant children went to their own. Carl and I were left behind. Why we weren't allowed to go home I'll never know. My parents didn't protest my having to sit in a classroom empty except for the teacher, who occasionally had me do busywork by myself. Carl did the same in another classroom.

One day I learned that Carl would be transferring to another school. My reaction was sheer terror. Now I really would be alone. I went home and shared my fear with my mother, who probably said the best thing possible in response to my situation. She assured me that not only was I just as good as anyone else, I was special. By this she meant not better than my peers but different in a positive way. Even at six I got it, and this affirmation helped me cope with my isolation.

My sister Linda, twenty at the time and a student at Syracuse University, recognized the disadvantages to me of remaining in the neighborhood and continuing to attend an inner-city school, so she decided to do something about it. In early 1955, she attended a party at a house in a well-manicured residential neighborhood that happened to be in the Nottingham High School district.

At that time there were eight high schools in Syracuse but only one where a very high percentage of students attended college. (When both sisters went there, the percentage was well over 90 percent; when I graduated in 1965, 88 percent of us went.) Nottingham's student body also was one-third Jewish, by far the highest Jewish student population in the city.

All of this added up in Linda's mind to her deciding that my parents should buy this home and thereby give me a greater chance at success. My parents were good people, but they were poor at making decisions like this on their own. To this day part of me envies kids who complain about "helicopter parents" who micromanage their lives. Academically speaking this approach sounds good to me, because as well-meaning as my parents were, they were totally lost when it came to advice about school. We moved in April of that year.

This was not the only crucial decision Linda made in loco parentis. At the same time she insisted that I be enrolled in Sunday school and Hebrew school. It is hard to imagine my parents neglecting my Jewish education, but Linda was the one who actually made the effort. Then she was gone. She married in July that same year, and sadly that void of guidance was unfilled by anyone else, except indirectly and to a limited degree by my highly motivated peers.

The remainder of my childhood and adolescence were relatively uneventful, which is no small thing. My Jewish upbringing continued. I became a Bar Mitzvah but then quit Hebrew school and was never confirmed. As far as I was concerned, continuing my Jewish education was irrelevant. Of course, I dutifully attended High Holy Day services with my father, a tradition I maintained most years until his death. I took my Jewishness for granted. It was never an issue partly because my parents supported an ecumenical life. We experienced no anti-Semitism, so there was no need to question my identity.

In high school I began to develop an interest in history, which I retain. In fact, I consider it a favorite hobby. It helped that I was surrounded by living history. For example, three of my uncles, one of whom I feature later, served overseas in World War II on both fronts. In addition, we lived across the street from a Greek immigrant family consisting of four boys and one girl. My mother befriended the girl, Joanne, and through her our families got on famously. My mother remained lifelong friends with Joanne. Her son John and I have done the same. He still is my oldest and dearest friend after seventy years.

From those relationships I got to know other "uncles" who also served during the war. So, in only two immigrant households, a total of seven boys served. Thankfully, they all returned safely, and there was a bounty of World War II memorabilia to keep John and me amused. My hard and unsentimental Uncle Leon even had two scrapbooks from that time that I would often look through and ask questions about. I remember five German medals he took off German prisoners of war whom he guarded (and abused) as an MP, his primary duty abroad. Leon could be difficult due to his intense racism, misogyny, and general insensitivity, but he never failed to answer my questions about the war. Because of the anti-Semitism he experienced firsthand while in Europe, I never comprehended why he couldn't empathize with the plight of African Americans in the United States. To him it was apples and concrete.

By far my favorite Greek "uncle" was Nick Constas, a big, bombastic, outrageous storyteller of the first order. As my mother's best friend's son John and I grew up, we realized that maybe all that Nick told us was a bit exaggerated. However, his stories were no less entertaining, and my favorite story he told is directly relevant to this narrative.

At the end of the war Nick was walking along a pier at an Italian port where ships with refugees or displaced persons were lined up for transit to America and elsewhere. Nick was completely fluent in Greek, and from one ship he heard singing in that language. Nick was the furthest thing from shy, so he boarded the ship, went below deck, and found a group of Greek Jews who had recently been liberated from concentration camps. One of them was a refugee from Salonika, Greece, which was home to a large Jewish community until World War II. Oddly the refugee's name was Albert Torres, which meant nothing to Nick at the time. In his mind, Mr. Torres was a Greek, Jew or not, with an odd name. Nick mixed in easily and for several hours boisterously shared in the survivors' celebration of liberation.

Fast-forward twenty-two years. Albert Torres had come to America, married a Hungarian Jewish refugee—also a survivor of the camps— settled down in Syracuse, and had two children, both of whom I knew. During the summer of 1967 I worked at a Jewish day camp where Mr. Torres's daughter Dora worked as well. We became friends, and one day I visited her at her home. Mr. Torres happened to be there, and I informed him of my connection to Nick Constas.

Nick had told of how two years earlier, in 1965, he was delivering cases of soda to a small diner named the CDM, which I think stood for the first names of Mr. Torres's wife and children. Nick carried a case on his shoulder through the front door and there stood the proprietor, Mr. Torres, who instantly recognized him and blurted out, "You Greek soldier."

What makes this story so compelling to me was the connection to Jewish history that this relationship embodied. Nineteen hundred years earlier, in 70 CE, the Romans had expelled Jews from the Holy Land, and one of the countries they landed in was Spain. Over the centuries a certain amount of acceptance, tolerance, and assimilation was prevalent, and many of the Jewish descendants adopted Spanish surnames like Torres.

In 1492 this golden era of Spanish Jewry ended under the reign of King Ferdinand and Queen Isabella, who with the complicity of the Catholic Church expelled hundreds of thousands of Jews around the Mediterranean: the ones who refused to convert. One of the welcoming countries was Greece, specifically Salonika, where Mr. Torres's ancestors settled. The Greeks were so tolerant and accepting that, unlike in other countries where Jews were forcibly resettled, they were permitted to keep their Spanish surnames.

Five hundred years later, Mr. Torres was one of the few survivors of the Diaspora and the Holocaust. I love this story because it ties two thousand years of Jewish history together with a person I actually knew. Mr. Torres was a proud Greek. He wore a Greek sailor's cap as long as I knew him, but he also retained his Jewish identity, which he passed on to his two children. What greater statement of Jewish resilience could there be?

Through personal stories and an examination of history, I came to understand my own identity and find strength in it. I did my best to offer up this practice to Greg in his new environment. In the following chapters I attempt to conjoin the basic elements of history, family, and love of country. By doing so I hope to develop and clarify a comprehensive context in which the overall purpose of this book can be considered.

It did not take long for Greg to run into an issue of religious intolerance. Shortly after the beginning of pilot training there was an incident at a social gathering at his home where another student made some unpleasant comments about Greg's Jewishness and walked out of the party. While the offending peer may have been acting from what he thought was being true to his faith, his comments, especially in the home of a host, were inappropriate.

In retrospect I may have overreacted to the incident, which Greg handled graciously. He is not a complainer and never used discrimination as an excuse. Greg and I had had talks over the years about how to handle anti-Semitic affronts. More recently and specifically, I had begun researching Jews in the military throughout history and passing along what I learned to Greg as a way to encourage, and—perhaps—as ammunition against anyone who might suggest that Jews did not belong. Greg is naturally thick skinned against personal insults, and what I offered him reinforced his resilience when confronted with intolerance.

I am pleased to report that throughout the entire course of Greg's training, there were no other major incidents. In spite of the presence of active Christian Evangelicals, particularly at the Air Force Academy, the Air Force in general does not endorse harassing non-Christians. Rather they uphold the tradition of religious tolerance as one of the principal values on which our great nation stands.

In fact, it has been abundantly clear that, since the Korean War, anti-Semitism in the US military is no longer institutional. Isolated incidents do occur, however, and no one should be surprised when they do.

In my first letter to Greg, my choice of a partisan was no accident because this remarkable man rose above the brutal Nazi anti-Semitism that surrounded him in occupied Poland and was able to lead an inspiring revolt against all odds. He proved that there were a substantial number of Jews who did not, as is sometimes said, go like sheep to the slaughter.

05/16/2005

Dear Greg,

I truly am sorry that I was right about the anti-Semitism that you might have to endure and may have to again. It is so ingrained in some, including those in the military, that it may always be a challenge for Jewish soldiers and airmen to cope with. As we talked about there is little if anything one can do about it except show them that you are just as good if not better than most (which we know to be the truth). In fact they may inadvertently make it easier for you by giving you extra incentive. Hold your ground about Judaism and remember that you are now part of a tradition of Jewish military service who have consistently served well in whatever country they were in, in spite of the bullshit they had to endure. Don't be surprised if you have to do a little bit better than some of your historic counterparts. When you do, your example will alter some of your peers' thinking, but unfortunately, not all of them. But then we can't do anything about this group who put their misplaced faith above their duty to their country and fail to honor the traditions of freedom of religion.

It bothers me about your being alone, and I know that the historical reasons for your relative isolation don't amount to much. At times when you need to, remember the military traditions (starting with the Maccabees) through the centuries up to the present. You are not alone, because the spirit of these fighters is in you (which is the main reason I liked the call name "Hammer" for you). Now you know. And while you are considering this, don't forget your brothers in arms in Israel who descend from the same tradition. If not for a quirk of historical fate, you could easily be flying for and kicking ass in the Israeli Air Force.

Anyway, I know you can handle the creeps because you stand on solid footing. Don't hesitate to use your faith to help you manage the times of spiritual confrontation (we were first!) and isolation. It's ironic to consider the fact that religious intolerance is in the mindset of some in the military ironically charged to protect democracy and the rights of the minority as they manifest their ignorance. At least your values are consistent and will serve you well throughout your career. They will help you blow off religious intolerance with ease.

Keep up the good work and remember we love you.

Love, Norm

Mordechai Anielewicz

Mordechai Anielewicz was one of the first Jews to recognize the Nazi threat to the very existence of the Jewish people when they came to power in the early to mid-1930s. After the German invasion of Poland in 1939, Anielewicz's considerable leadership skills transformed a nonviolent underground youth organization into an armed resistance movement. At the time there was controversy in the Jewish ghetto community regarding the appropriate response to Nazi oppression. Some thought that cooperation would at least buy time and give a lucky few a chance for survival. Anielewicz did not equivocate and went about preparing his followers for the inevitable violent confrontation.

Mordechai Anielewicz deserves a special place among Jewish military heroes because he could have avoided certain death when he escaped from Warsaw in 1942. However, he chose to return to the ghetto later that year and discovered that only 60,000 of the 350,000 Jews who were there when he left remained. Rather than passively await deportation and certain death, Anielewicz built the Jewish Combat Organization from among the survivors and prepared to resist.

In November 1942, Anielewicz was appointed commander of a combined resistance force and awaited a final deportation and emptying of the ghetto. On April 19, 1943, the Germans entered the ghetto for what they thought would be a routine roundup. Instead, the Jewish Combat Organization fiercely fought back.

Heavy casualties were inflicted on the Nazis, who were forced to bring in crack troops to put down the revolt. The Jews held out against tremendous odds until May 8, 1943, when Anielewicz and most of his defenders were killed in the final assault on their bunker at Mila 18.

Mordechai Anielewicz's dream of creating a Jewish self-defense force had become a reality. His efforts and those of his fellow resistance fighters served as an inspiration to other Jews in similar desperate circumstances to fight and die with dignity rather than passively capitulate.

In a last letter to a friend, Anielewicz wrote on April 23, 1943, "The most important thing is that my life's dream has come true. Jewish self-defense in the ghetto has been realized. Jewish retaliation and resistance has been fact. I have been witness to the magnificent heroic battle of the Jewish fighter."

•

Early into flight training, Greg's resolve was tested. Although he managed the technical side of training quite well, the hazing was taking a toll on his life. While hazing in the Army and Marine Corps during basic training is well known, what pilot candidates go through is less well understood. Frequently and without warning, students are "stood up" before an instructor inches away and required under intense duress to respond to detailed, highly technical questions. Failure to respond quickly enough or appropriately is consequential to the student's status and progress.

My relationship with Greg was solid enough for him to feel comfortable expressing his frustrations, which seemed to help. Soon afterward he was returning to his old self, but better, stronger, and wiser from his experiences. I thought at this time that a great allied WWII hero would be a proper inspiration, one about whom most Jews know nothing.

06/01/2005

Dear Greg,

Relatively speaking I think you are doing quite well. I'm not just saying that glibly— I think I know you well enough to under- stand what is going on. The mental/emotional tricks to coping with this type of chal- lenge are to lower your expectations to reasonable levels. Don't personalize the hazing, and reality-test your situation when you start beating yourself up. By reality test I mean put this unpleasant experience in perspective, which will prevent the negativity from getting the best of you. I'm sure you already know this but as with everything worthwhile it takes practice, and the mental side of your training may be more important than the practical side.

I also wanted to convey one other thing. Although I have always been and always will be a huge supporter, don't confuse this with blind ambition by proxy. If at any time you decide to leave the program, I'm sure that it will be for the right reasons and I will support that decision. In other words don't worry about disappointing me. You could never do that.

You have some disadvantages that the other guys don't have, such as your non-military background—so this challenge is real and I don't perceive you as whining. In fact, to verbalize as openly as you do and to have a wife like Shana to verbalize to is a distinct advantage over your peers.

Yes the pressures are enormous but so are the rewards that you may not be fully aware of yet. *Fighter Pilot* [Robin Olds's book] described a few of these rewards very well. All I know is that whatever price you pay will be well worth it and you will have your old life back to boot in 2-3 short years.

So keep your good eyes on the prize, keep
your balance (hopefully using us, whenever
necessary) and good things will happen.

Love, Norm

David Dragunsky

History confirms the fact that World War II would have been an even greater struggle for the United States had it not been for the Soviet Union. From a Jewish perspective, as many Jews (500,000) fought on the Eastern Front as were in the American armed forces. The vast majority of Jewish combat deaths, 212,000 out of a total of 270,000, occurred in this theater of war. Unfortunately, Cold War politics and propaganda prevented proper credit from being given to our Russian ally and its Jewish soldiers, but history can't be changed. Sgt. David Dragunsky was a Russian tank driver who took part in some of the most decisive battles of the war. As the conflict progressed, he commanded a tank company, battalion, and brigade in rapid succession. He is best known in military annals for becoming a Hero of the Soviet Union, the Russian equivalent of the US Medal of Honor, on not one but two occasions. This feat was matched by only a handful of Red Army combatants. Dragunsky survived the war and was eventually promoted to the rank of colonel general (the equivalent of our four-star), one of twenty-seven Jews who became general officers in the Russian Army during the course of World War II.

•

I never doubted for an instant that Greg would accomplish his goal. In the following letter I took the opportunity, as I did on several other occasions later, to reference his faith as a source of strength in times of adversity. I tried hard not to patronize him, but at the same time I

wanted to come across as unequivocally and unquestionably supportive, which is the least a parent can do.

The hero of this week's story is interesting because he displays
Jewish loyalty to Israel even at great inconvenience to his own personal
life. My point to Greg was to reinforce the idea that a patriotic loyal
American does not compromise his values by honoring a commitment
to one's people.

06/08/2005

Dear Greg,

I was pleased to hear you sound more like
your old self. Not that I was worried or
anything but the parent keeps coming out
in me. Imagine that.

It's easy for me to think this way, but
when you tell me how tough you have it in
training I mostly have positive thoughts.
First and foremost I'm proud of you for
your tenacity, which has to be one of the
reasons they picked you in the first place.
When you finish you will know that you
accomplished something few would have even
qualified for. Your innate abilities, which
some would call gifts from God, are not
being wasted away. The Talmud teaches that
we are judged not just on what we do in our
lives but also whether we have fulfilled
whatever potential we have. You will be
able to look at yourself in a mirror and
know that you gave it your all.

Second, I feel a sense of security
knowing that the training will increase

dramatically your ability to survive adversity. I'm talking about mental stress as much as if not more than physical stress. I know that it's hard if not impossible to have this perspective at this phase of your training but I'm sure you will later.

I know that the best is yet to come, and that overall you will relish your years in the Guard. It won't be long. Aren't you about at week #10 already?

Have fun during your solo. You have always done better when you do tough things alone. Again, the Air Force knew what they were doing when they picked you. Believe it!

Love, Norm

Mickey Marcus

Mickey Marcus could easily have been cited as a hero for his participation in World War II as an American army officer. After being named the commandant of the US Army's new Ranger school in 1942, he was sent to England on the eve of D-Day. There he parachuted into Normandy with the 101st Airborne Division. However, he is best remembered for his military leadership with the nascent State of Israel.

Near the end of the war, Marcus's consciousness as a Jew was awakened when he was put in charge of cleaning out the death camps and sustaining the recently liberated millions of starving survivors. While in postwar Europe, he came to comprehend the depths of European anti-Semitism. The need for a Jewish homeland in Palestine for the remnants of European Jewry became clear to him.

Shortly after the war, Marcus volunteered to assist Israel as a military adviser. He developed a command structure for the new army, wrote training manuals, and adapted his Ranger experience to the Israelis' special needs.

Marcus's guerrilla tactics were used to break the Arab siege of Jerusalem, helped bring about an Israeli victory, and provided border security for the new state. In gratitude, David Ben-Gurion, Israel's first prime minister, named Marcus the first general in the army of Israel since the Diaspora two thousand years before. Ben-Gurion simply said of him, "He was the best man we had."

CHAPTER 2

Say Little

"Say little and do much."

—Jewish proverb

JEWS ARE OVERREPRESENTED IN THE HEALTH professions not because we are smarter than other ethnic groups but because education is so highly valued. I remember reading some years ago that 28 percent of physicians were Jewish even though Jews represented only 2 percent of the population at that time.

So of course becoming a medical professional was expected of me. My uncle Nat, the youngest of my father's eight brothers and sisters, was the only one to go to college. His siblings had pitched in to send him to New York University and then Jefferson Medical College in Philadelphia. He in turn felt obligated to take care of them, my father included.

Nat died at sixty-one of a heart attack. In his will he left a significant sum of money for Phyllis and me to attend college. At five years old I recall saying to Nat that I too would be a doctor.

I would describe my adolescence as years of high expectations with low parental participation. My "support" mostly derived from my high-achieving peers whose parents were able to assist actively with their education and their futures.

As a result, I went through high school using those around me to lead the way. This lack of a clear focus combined with my inherent unwillingness to push myself to excellence resulted in mediocre grades, low standardized test scores, and no clue as to how to translate these basic realities into a college choice.

While my peers were striving for the Ivy League, I was content to settle for a lesser degree of intensity—not that any Ivy League school would have considered me. This pattern of underachievement and occasional laziness continued through college and nearly derailed my career.

The only thing I knew upon applying to college was that I wanted the adventure of leaving home and not to go to Syracuse University. Such a school would have been great—if it were somewhere else. I applied to three schools, was rejected by my first choice, and decided to attend the University of Pittsburgh. My erratic study habits plagued me for the next four years. Any aspiration to become a physician evaporated my freshman year when I failed basic chemistry.

Upon hearing this, my father was disappointed and angry. Woe to me if Nat had been alive then. In Pop's mind, anything less than being a medical doctor would leave me vulnerable to the whims of others. I would be stripped of the prestige and money that go along with a profession less susceptible to anti-Semitic forces, an attitude my father understandably brought with him from Eastern Europe. He never completely recovered from this disappointment, in spite of the considerable success I had as a psychologist.

My lack of discipline for study was reinforced by my unlikely and unforeseen career in collegiate athletics. Sports weren't everything in our household, but they were fairly important. Hank Greenberg and Sandy Koufax were Jewish heroes and role models to us because they stood up for their beliefs and proudly but quietly wore their Jewishness. However, in my family they were not aspirational figures, and no one expected serious athletics to be any part of my future.

The only "athletic" memory I have of my father was when I was ten. We were walking to a beach not far from a summer cottage my parents bought on Oneida Lake. On the way I decided to have a little fun with the old man. He was over sixty at the time, and I thought I had pretty decent speed.

I challenged him to a race, thinking that he would be no match. At first he resisted, so I began trash-talking about how badly I would beat him. I was full of myself that day, thinking that this would be a gross mismatch. Plus he was wearing sandals and I had on sneakers.

Finally, he had enough of my guff and it was ready, set, go. I didn't have a chance. Pop blew by me as if I were standing still. In a way, even then I was proud of him. He never rubbed it in.

Since both sisters had attended Syracuse University, I grew up bleeding orange for the Orangemen of Syracuse. Fifi took me to many football games where we sat in the student section. There I was imbued with student spirit.

Some of my fondest memories are attending games on a bright, sunny October day. The beautiful Syracuse campus would be on fire with the colors of fall, and the air cool and crisp. The crowd's anticipation was electric. I was hooked.

Uncle Odie worked at a bar called the Clover Club, which catered mostly to Syracuse students, including football players. Being the warm and generous man that he was, "Pudge" invited a few of them to our house for home-cooked meals. I so looked forward to those meals because I was awestruck by these guys who had won a national championship in 1959.

I was in a family of fans but not participants. Playing was for others, and I was never encouraged to take part in sports. So when the players came to dinner, I would drag them into the backyard and play catch with real athletes. They always accommodated me while my sports-minded father and uncles never gave a second thought about leaving me on the sidelines. My athletic experience consisted of playing pickup games with a host of good friends until I decided to get serious at the advanced age of fifteen.

I grew up loving baseball, but I had no youth league experience. Seriously, who would have taken me to practices and games?

At fifteen I thought I'd quit being a mere spectator and on my own try organized baseball. Two years of summer ball and one year on the high school team were minimal preparation for playing at a higher level. At that point I would have been quite content to extend my academic mediocrity until graduation. Only later would I worry about a career.

Suddenly my life was turned upside down, and my chance of taking my studies seriously disappeared in a flash.

Shortly after college began in the fall of 1965, I was playing racquetball on the Pitt campus. The court had an observation area above and behind it. I didn't notice who my audience was until after I finished my set. As I was leaving the court, I was approached by none other than the head soccer coach and an assistant.

Without further ado, the coach, Leo Bemis, inquired as to whether I would be interested in learning how to play soccer. Really? I quickly replied that there were no soccer programs in Syracuse, including at the high school level. I had never kicked a soccer ball in my life. Coach was undeterred. He pressed the issue, so I agreed. I was pulled from physical education class and introduced to this strange new sport.

The offer might not have seemed so attractive had the Pitt team been lame. They weren't. They were in the midst of a run that would carry them to the NCAA Sweet Sixteen and a national ranking. Pitt was led by a bona fide All-American, George Sommer; a player named Vince Bartolotta, who would get an Olympic alternate spot; and several other scholarship athletes who had played the sport much of their lives.

I had no recollection of what they saw in me, but all of a sudden I was immersed in the world of Division I athletics. After sitting on the bench as a baseball player for the past three years, hungry for playing time and recognition, I was handed a chance to be in the spotlight.

I was introduced to my very first soccer game, which I will never forget. As I said, the team was excellent and was drawing attention. Fans lined the field on all sides, cheering wildly for their guys. I was smitten and agreed to become part of the freshman team.

The freshman coach, Bob McNulty—the best coach I ever had— took me aside and taught me the basics, that is, what a five-year-old would learn. I was no prodigy, but I gradually caught on. I even got to play a little on the undefeated freshman team, so when I was invited to advance to the varsity the following year, there was no hesitation. Studies be damned!

I learned the hard way about the importance of setting proper priorities. In spite of ongoing concerns about my consistently low GPA, I gave no thought to the future and played on. I can't say for certain if not playing would have made a big difference, given my subpar academic history, but soccer was much more important to my fragile ego.

Nothing has been cooler in my life than going to an away game and representing my school. I was given a trainer-packed bag with all the essentials and dressed in a classic blue blazer with the Pitt pocket crest, gray slacks, white shirt, and gold-and-blue-striped tie. Stepping off the team bus on a strange college campus was exhilarating, and I couldn't get enough of it.

By my senior year my skills had progressed to the point where I received considerably more playing time. However, a painful incident served to rudely remind me of my Jewish identity.

I had spent much of the summer prior to my senior year working on my soccer skills. Unfortunately, this was done at the expense of conditioning, and I reported to two-a-days relatively out of shape.

The new assistant coach, the aforementioned Vince Bartolotta, had graduated, gone to the Marine Officers Candidate School, and returned to assume his new position. He rightfully had no tolerance for the physical state I was in, and one day he literally dragged me around the field to complete my laps. In retrospect I know I deserved this and didn't push back. However, this coach shortly thereafter crossed a line.

By this time, I was the only Jew left on the team. When the High Holy Days approached, I would always inform the coach that I would be unavailable on those days. I remember attending services on the Day of Atonement but then going to the game to root on my team-mates. However, I refused to play. If Hank Greenberg and Sandy Koufax wouldn't play, I wasn't about to either.

One practice shortly thereafter I was struggling with my sprints when the coach derided me by reminding me that it was no longer Yom Kippur. For some reason his insensitivity flew all over me and I told him to fuck himself in front of the entire team and head coach, who was utterly appalled at my comment. Vinny could have said anything else as a reprimand, personal or otherwise, and I would have taken it, but this I couldn't and wouldn't accept.

I was ashamed of myself because I really liked Vinny and could have managed the situation more tactfully. I didn't, and I expected to be dismissed from the team. I wasn't.

Vinny came to me to apologize, which I gratefully accepted, and I did the same. We made up and remained friends. Shortly thereafter, I was promoted to the starting team. As with my initial involvement, I never learned why. I was elated by the news and determined to prove that I belonged. I think I did because after my being named a starter, we finished the season successfully and I earned my much-desired letter jacket.

Unfortunately, my letter was more important to me than my education. As a sophomore, I had had to declare a major. I chose psychology largely because of an eccentric character I used to philosophize with about the human condition. This very funny guy would take out his tobacco-less pipe, sit back, and talk authoritatively about behavior theory as if he were someone other than a lowly undergrad. However, as misguided as these debates certainly were, they were stimulating and piqued my interest. I gradually came to see myself in the role of a psychologist. However, by the time I figured this out, my mediocre undergraduate grades weren't close to what were required to get into graduate school. I again only made average scores on the Graduate Record Exam and was summarily rejected by every doctoral program to which I applied.

Looking back, it was presumptuous and arrogant of me to think that I was a viable candidate. Since only a handful of students are accepted into psychology training programs, the odds can be daunting: thirty-to-one or higher. I had no chance in hell. I was going to have to do it the hard way.

I graduated from the University of Pittsburgh in 1969. Without a plan I returned to Syracuse and was promptly drafted but found medically unfit for military service. While relieved at the time, I experienced a measure of self-reproach because many of my friends did serve in the Vietnam War, and most paid a price.

One of them was my Greek friend, John, who I think felt pressure from his uncles' service and answered the call. Because he was a good friend, he never held my not going against me, nor did any of my uncles on either side. But part of me still feels ashamed. Since then, I assuaged some of the guilt by devoting a significant part of my practice to helping vets from several conflicts who developed post-traumatic stress disorder (PTSD).

One week after I got home, I took a job in an aluminum casting foundry. It was a hot, dusty, grimy, and noisy place to work. Since it was a nonunion shop, many of the workers were ex-convicts who were having difficulty finding work elsewhere. As is my way, I got along with everyone and was even offered a foreman's position.

Working there made me realize that I needed to do something different with my life. Desperation is a great motivator, and I wasn't about to embarrass myself in front of my family and peers. In 1970, three months after quitting the job, I begged my way into a master's program at Syracuse University. A professor saw my potential and gave me a chance in spite of my grades, and I'll always be grateful to him for believing in me. The day I stepped back onto a campus, I felt like I had come home. While I was in school, I was hired as a social worker and racked my brain to figure out a way to get into a doctoral program. My grades improved, I secured solid recommendations, and in 1971 I applied and was admitted to Boston University, where I started working toward becoming a psychologist.

In my first year at BU, I worked harder academically than I ever had, and in spring 1972 I was admitted to the doctoral dissertation track. I did not understand at the time that the first year of the program was a qualifying period after which only some of us would be allowed to progress to the doctorate. The others would be relegated to a terminal degree short of being allowed to call themselves psychologists.

Between 1972 and my graduation in 1977 I was out of sorts. As I approached the completion of my studies, I became anxious and confused because I really had no direction beyond the degree. As a result, what should have taken three years to finish took six, at the end of which I was truly floundering. These concluding years of my doctoral program were the worst years of my life, worse than when I was faced later with life-threatening cancer. I was depressed, with significant suicidal ideation, anxious to the point of having severe panic attacks, and lost regarding any future course. I sought counseling, which was ineffectual partly because no medication relief was ever suggested. At the same time, I had drifted away from my faith and did not have spiritual access to it for grounding and regrouping.

A book pulled me out of my funk. I don't remember the details, but I do remember picking up a volume on Jewish history that I had seen on my middle sister's bookshelf. I hadn't read it then, but this time I devoured it. I distinctly remember getting back some spiritual footing.

During those awful eighteen months I decided to sharpen my Jewish identity by giving up all pork and shellfish. (Living in Boston made this sacrifice all the more difficult.) I have maintained this dietary restriction since then with no regrets. It can seem like a small thing, even arbitrary today, but there is no way I can go into a seafood or Chinese restaurant and not remind myself of who I am.

After finally completing my doctoral studies and following many years of continuous and intense work as a mental health professional, I joined a friend for a cruise in 1986. This was when Greg, Carol, and I started to be become a family. At that time, I had been a psychologist for a decade, specializing in individual, family, and institutional crisis interventions. I had been on the front lines in New Hampshire during multiple difficult situations. When the space shuttle *Challenger* blew up on takeoff, carrying with it teacher Christa McAuliffe, I went to her high school to counsel the students and staff. From countless violent domestic disputes to dealing with a variety of angry people embroiled in the various storms of life, I had been there and I knew when I needed a break. Little did I know that on my break I would meet the love of my life and my son. The fact that at first Carol didn't like me and asked to switch tables so as not to have to endure a shrink for the entire trip did nothing to dissuade me. Luckily, it didn't take long for Carol and me to connect and for me to bond with Greg.

In 1988, I moved from Concord, New Hampshire, to Houston, Texas, where we expected to eventually settle. However, after much deliberation I thought it best to move to Lubbock, so that Greg could remain close to his father. I joined them in 1990, starting my private practice in this moderately sized West Texas town of limited diversity. I decided long before I met Carol and Greg that I wanted a Jewish home when I married. I never wanted my own children, but I was never against raising stepchildren. I'd seen such a marvelous example of inclusion from my sister Phyllis, who raised her husband's two small children along with their three biological children, that I didn't worry about it at all. I got my wish for a Jewish wife, a Jewish household, and a bonus child. I had long before promised myself to raise at least one child who would continue the Jewish tradition. Greg is that child. Phyllis also taught me about character. Shortly before our mother died, she gave her wedding ring to Phyllis and told her to give it to me when I married. Phyllis never said a word about it for thirteen years, but when the time came, she gave it to me to give to my beloved Carol.

Being Jewish in a small city can be tough. There are about 100 confirmed Jews in this town of 250,000 and one small synagogue to serve the community. Carol and I were determined to raise Greg as a Jew to the best of our abilities. We became active members at the synagogue and celebrated all holidays. I helped Greg with his Bar Mitzvah studies, including Hebrew instruction, and kept him in Sunday school through confirmation at age sixteen. Carol and I are very proud that Greg is raising his children, Abby and Sam, in a Jewish home as well.

Throughout his life, Greg had to explain aspects of Judaism— such as the festival of Hanukkah—to his classmates upon request from his teachers. Due to Hanukkah's proximity to Christmas, Gentiles have elevated what had been a very minor holiday to the Jewish people. In junior high school Greg was sent home one day with a sheet of paper with a warning about students possibly wearing Satanic symbols. I was shocked to see that one of the "devil's markings" was the Star of David. It was beyond Carol and me how this misconception could have ever passed under the radar.

At the time, Greg wore a mezuzah around his neck, which was visible. Fortunately, before any disciplinary actions could be taken, we immediately responded to the school, which realized its mistake. As with their annual disregard for the High Holy Days, on which exams inevitably were scheduled, we tried not to make a big deal about these oversights. We didn't want to have our issues discounted by being labeled as chronic complainers. However, we did this in full knowledge that we'd have our sensibilities offended

Bill Keith in West Texas.   Opal Keith in her WAVES uniform .

annually, which is in fact what happened. Greg graduated from high school in 1996 and then attended the University of Texas, where his Jewish identity coexisted comfortably with that of over four thousand other Jewish students among a total population of forty thousand.

Being in relative isolation has proved to be frustrating, illuminating, and a testimony to what my co-religionists have had to confront on a much greater scale. Having a Jewish home, a loving family, and a supportive community made this isolation more tolerable.

However, Greg did not have to look far to find inspiration for patriotism and military service. Greg's own maternal grandmother, Opal Keith, was a member of the first regiment of Navy WAVES (Women Accepted for Volunteer Emergency Service) recruited at the beginning of World War II. Incidentally, after the initial push into Germany, her

Gen. James Breedlove climbing into F4.

husband, Bill Keith, was captured in 1945 and made a POW for three months until he was freed at the war's end.

Greg has been blessed not only with his extended family and their histories as examples but also with many influential friends who served their country in the armed forces. Gen. James Breedlove stands out most prominently among them. Jim was a personal friend of the family. He served as an inspiration for Greg in a way that none of the rest of us could. Gen. Breedlove flew more than two hundred combat missions over Korea and Vietnam and was awarded the Distinguished Flying Cross among many other medals for his exemplary service. His confidence in Greg from the beginning was unwavering even when Greg was struggling the most. Gen. Breedlove's reaction was always the same: not to worry, the Air Force will not give up on someone who has all the potential of becoming a good fighter pilot.

I have to admit that Jim had a problem with this book project when I told him about it early in its development. He disliked the concept of hyphenated Americans, Jews included, because he strongly thought that all prejudicial nonsense should disappear once someone put on an American uniform. I have no doubt that under *his* command this was the case. Unfortunately, history reminds us that the story of all too many hyphenated Americans who served their country needed to be told.

•

Having lived in a southern state, especially one with as proud a military history as Texas, made my discovery of a Jewish Confederate officer that much more interesting. He was highlighted in a book titled *Jews of the Confederacy*, part of which detailed Jewish military contributions during the Civil War.

The obvious irony of a Jew fighting for a country that sought to preserve the institution of slavery when Jews themselves were in fact slaves in Egypt makes this subject a hard one for most Jews to swallow. However, the point of including him was to emphasize the Talmudic directive that a Jew was required to fight for his country. They may not always agree with the principles being defended, but Jews, like anyone else, got the call and responded, sometimes with remarkable heroism, like this southern gentleman. His men loved and revered him—and referred to him as the "Jew Major."

06/13/2005

Dear Greg,

I was at dinner the other night at a public event and of course the conversation swung around to Jews in the military. When I told the guests about the next Jewish military figure of significance I would be sending to you, a Confederate officer, one of the comments was, "Sounds like an oxymoron." Ignorance rears its ugly head again, i.e., the assumption that Jews would not or could not (out of cowardice) fight for, in this case, the Southern cause. (Surely, it wasn't that he thought there were no Jews in the South at that time.)

This is not anti-Semitism per se, but this type of ignorance perpetuates what you will have to face during your commitment. Personally, I love the fact that your presence beats down the stereotype of weak, cowardly and anti-physical Jews. People can minimize or even negate our contributions but they can't deny your reality. Every person you will meet will have to accept the fact that you have accomplished something few others have and there's no way to rationalize your achievement by assuming that strings were pulled. The difficulty of your training rules out nepotism, i.e., no one who flies an F-16 doesn't merit respect and admiration, begrudging as it may be.

I know that this is an extra burden for

you to represent our people in this way but
there is no getting around it. However, if
you think about the pride involved as well
as the historical precedent, this burden
can transform into a tremendous asset. You
don't even have to say a word, just be! And
the statement will be made.

The men whose names I'm sending you,
most had to endure this particular form of
anti-Semitism stereotype. They all survived
and accounted extremely well of themselves
as Jews and as soldiers, seamen and airmen.
You have now joined their pantheon so let
their strength be your strength.

Love, Norm

Adolph Proskauer

The notion of Jew versus Jew in armed combat is a difficult reality
for Jews to accept. History has so commonly thrust the Jewish people
in this role of minority underdog that it took until relatively modern
times for Jews to be in a position to confront each other as representatives of warring countries. However, Jews did fight and kill each other
in countless wars, not the least of which was the American Civil War.

Major Adolph Proskauer, a native of Mobile, Alabama, was
wounded in three major Civil War battles, but at the Battle of
Gettysburg he distinguished himself as a consummate warrior. There,
he led the 12th Alabama Regiment in a valiant but losing battle.
During the fight he gained enormous respect from those who served
under him because of his courage under fire.

Ironically, Frederick Knefler, a Union general, led Northern
soldiers at the same battle. It would have been fascinating to learn

of their respective perspectives as Jews in combat against each other if they had had a chance to meet and discuss their experiences. Both survived the war and lived long lives as leaders amid their respective Jewish communities in Alabama and Indiana.

•

The next letter I wrote was composed just prior to Greg's first solo flight. He had struggled, as most pilot candidates do, with the extremely rigorous physical and psychological demands of the Undergraduate Pilot Training program. In keeping with the spirit of this project designed to reinforce his spiritual identity and provide strength during stressful times, I had been reflecting on the time in my life when I was the only Jew in my elementary school, forced to sit in a room by myself while the other children received religious instruction at their own houses of worship.

I considered the letters to be an opportunity for Greg to get to know me better (and vice versa). As it turned out, he had never heard the story in the nineteen years I had known him.

It was also an appropriate time to tell the story of Alfred Dreyfus. While I had no evidence that his faith helped him cope with the ordeal of Devil's Island and the virulent French anti-Semitism at the time, Dreyfus never renounced his Judaism nor blamed it for his problems. His quiet endurance was inspirational.

06/23/2005

Dear Greg,

As you approach your solo flight I am anxious for you to have this correspondence.

As you know I think about you a lot, and every once in a while a memory flashes into my head that you may find helpful in coping with your spiritual isolation. I'm not sure if you recall that for nearly the first 3 years of school, K–2, I was the only Jew in a school of well over a thousand baby boomers. Being the only Jew was never intimidating to me. Rather I have welcomed the challenge and took pride in my ability to blend but remain separate. Many times I was the only Jew on the athletic teams I participated with. I didn't wear my Jewishness as a challenge to others but I never hid it and I tried to educate my peers whenever they were open to new input. I went through exactly the same demands as anyone else and I hope that by example I dismissed a few negative stereotypes. My success at coping remains a source of pride for me and allowed me to adapt well in relatively Jew-less parts of the country like Concord, NH or Lubbock, TX. These experiences only made me stronger, not weaker.

I know that you will respond at least as well as I did and even better. Acting non-plussed or indifferent when confronted by ignorance infuriates proselytes because this behavior makes a statement about the solidity of your beliefs.

Love, Norm

Alfred Dreyfus

Alfred Dreyfus, a captain at the time, was the center of a situation in France in 1894 that came to be known as the Dreyfus Affair. When evidence was found that indicated that French military intelligence was being funneled to the Germans, suspicions fell on Capt. Dreyfus. Not only did he have access to the communications in question, he was also a Jew.

Dreyfus was found guilty of treason during a secret military trial during which he was denied the right to examine the "evidence" against him. He was subsequently stripped of his rank and sent to Devil's Island, an infamous penal colony off the north coast of South America, with a sentence of life imprisonment. The French extreme right used the incident as proof of Jewish treachery. However, once exonerated four years later, rather than quit in disgust, Dreyfus served with distinction in combat as a line officer during World War I.

•

In the next letter I included my uncle Leon Margolis's dog tags and a little anecdote about him.

"Anti-Semitism" may be too strong a word to use about the Air Force's support of evangelism, particularly at the Air Force Academy. Well-meaning religious intolerance is probably a much better description. Nonetheless, it can be distracting and bothersome and requires one to be on guard about unwelcome evangelizing. An investigation at the Air Force Academy into excessive proselytizing by evangelical members of the military toward non-Christians led to an unsatisfactory slap on their collective wrists.

This week's subject is an MSNBC analyst on military issues who used his Judaism to help inspire him to the action that led to his receipt of the Medal of Honor. He recalled in his memoirs that just prior to engaging in his heroic acts, he quickly reflected on the Jewish adage that goes, "If I am only for myself, who am I? If I am not for others, what am I? And if not now, when?"

While Greg is a true team player, his desire to fly a single-seat fighter never changed. Once he accomplished this lifelong dream he quickly understood why it had been so important to him. Just ask any fighter pilot.

06/28/2005

Dear Greg,

Enclosed is a little WWII memorabilia. My uncle was no war hero. In fact he lost his stripes on not one but two occasions. The significance of these tags regarding the general theme of these letters is that at least on one of the occasions when he was busted in rank was for fighting with Jew baiters. I'm certainly not advocating that you get physical with anyone but there are limits as to how much crap we have to take.

Too bad not more was done to the A.F. Academy evangelists. I hope they cut the non-Christians as much slack in their efforts to be left alone to observe their faiths without interference.

Congratulations on your solo success. It was easy to lose sight of so obvious a factor to your happiness as flying by yourself. But that is the outcome, and training is a small price to pay for such a great opportunity. Here's to your next solo—and beyond.

Kinky Friedman is in town today, and David Bass and I are going to see him. I'll ask him if he's looking for another fine Texas Jew to be in his cabinet someday . . . you know who. He's dead serious about his candidacy. I wonder if the

```
Republicans will go after him if they are
threatened in the slightest way. Can you be
a Jew and a Texan at the same time?
                              Love, Norm
```

Jack Jacobs

Col. Jack Jacobs, MSNBC military analyst, distinguished himself on March 8, 1968, as an assistant battalion adviser to a South Vietnamese Army division. During an assault on a Viet Cong position, the company commander became disabled, and then-Capt. Jacobs assumed command of the allied company in spite of being wounded by a mortar.

Without regard for his personal safety, Capt. Jacobs made repeated trips across fire-swept open paddies to evacuate several wounded troops. In the process he drove off multiple enemy assaults. He was credited with saving the lives of fourteen allied soldiers and preventing the defeat of his fighting unit.

•

In the past Greg had expressed an interest in going into politics one day, so I wanted to keep him informed about the activities of Kinky Friedman—irreverent country rock musician, prolific mystery novel author, owner of an animal rescue ranch, and a candidate for the governor of Texas. Kinky creates ways to combine his Jewish and Texas roots in a manner that both groups find approachable and humorous.

```
                                       07/05/2005

Dear Greg,

Enclosed is an article about Kinky's appear-
ance in Lubbock last week. He really is
```

quite funny and he's not afraid to flash his Jewish roots. For example, the first thing he'd do as Governor would be to honor his heritage and reduce the speed limit to $54.95. Then he'd appoint Willie Nelson as Energy Czar and head of the Texas Rangers. Carol and I agreed to not vote in the primaries so that we can sign a petition to get him on the ballot. He hired Jesse Ventura's campaign manager so who knows? In any event he will shake things up in Austin where they are doing their best to ignore him.

Carol and I visited Jim (Gen. Breedlove) on July 4th weekend. He is frail but fit and his mind is as sharp as ever. He is very pleased and proud of your progress in flight school and he said what everyone else said of your loving the T-38. This should ease any doubt you had about your decision. I'm sure that he would like to talk with you anytime. He has so many interesting stories, one of which I'm anxious to share with you because of its relevance to your future.

Love, Norm

Benjamin Kauffman

During World War I, Jews had their version of Sgt. York in Sgt. Benjamin Kauffman. While Sgt. York tricked the enemy into exposing their positions by imitating turkey sounds, Sgt. Kauffman used a different kind of bluff to achieve notoriety. After having his arm shattered by a bullet, he single-handedly advanced on a machine gun position with a few grenades and an empty pistol.

Sgt. Kauffman captured the position and returned to his friendly line. With resistance eliminated, the Americans were able to advance. For his heroism, Sgt. Kauffman was awarded the Medal of Honor, one of three Jews so decorated during World War I.

A Jew Must Defend

"A Jew must defend the country in which he lives."

—The Talmud

WHILE I KNEW RELATIVELY EARLY IN LIFE THAT I would never be a biological father, I never backed away from the idea of being a stepparent. However, I was unprepared for some of the unforeseeable anxieties of parenting. Shortly after I moved from Houston to Lubbock in 1990, Greg, now age twelve, was practicing rappelling off a wooden play structure in the backyard. He had inadvertently failed to secure a proper knot on the support rope. As he descended, the rope suddenly snapped. When he fell, he extended his arms behind him to break his fall and fractured both wrists. I was standing not twenty feet from him and watched helplessly.

Greg was in bilateral casts for six weeks, during which time he could do little for himself. Carol and I had to help him with or perform for him the most basic activities of daily living.

For me this incident was an introduction into the intricacies of child-rearing. There was no occasion to stand back and watch Carol do it all. She was busy working twelve hours a day supporting us while I built my practice, so I stepped in. I tried my best to balance our time between helping him with his studies, which now was the clear priority, and having "Disneyland time" together. We played all sorts of games—electronic and otherwise—went to lots of movies and sporting events, and often went out to eat by ourselves. Even though the circumstances of his injuries were unfortunate, the time we spent together that we otherwise would not have had strengthened our bond. A solid foundation was set and hardening as he approached adolescence.

The relationship between the Jewish people and military service has been complicated throughout history. As noted many times in the Bible, the Jewish nation had developed a warrior ethos and used its military prowess to conquer new lands and its many enemies. This warrior ethos was never better exemplified than by the Maccabees, who fought a three-year guerrilla war against Roman occupation and desecration of the Holy Temple in Jerusalem in the second century BC. The Maccabees, led by Judah the Hammer, briefly regained their nation before finally succumbing to the Romans. In 70 CE, after another war with the Romans, the Jews were expelled as a people in what became known as the Diaspora.[1] Subsequently they became a subjugated people totally dependent on their host countries for nearly two thousand years—first in pagan lands, which then largely became Christian after the fourth century and later Muslim after the seventh century.

Jews existed as a tiny minority who stubbornly refused to accept the religious ideology of the dominant religion. Discrimination became an inevitable consequence, and the long history of oppression and persecution began to shape the Jewish mindset. Burgeoning anti-Semitism affected every area of Jewish life: where they could

---

1 Martin Gilbert, *The Illustrated Atlas of Jewish Civilization* (New York: Macmillan, 1994), 45–47.

live, what livelihood they could pursue, how they could observe their faith, and more.

Jewish passivity in response to overwhelming dominance became a survival mechanism. Openly resisting persecution would have most certainly led to cultural suicide. Over the centuries anti-Semitism evolved into an international phenomenon based upon imagined Jewish conspiracies ranging from geopolitical movements such as communism and world finance to bizarre religious practices. International anti-Semitism reveals a fully developed and clearly articulated critical disposition toward Jews that extends beyond mere prejudice. In many countries, the United States as well, this broader worldview became institutionalized, including in the military, and had a direct effect on policy decisions.[2]

For example, after Jews became liable for military conscription in the Russian Empire in 1825, opportunities within the armed forces were very limited and almost no Jews could rise to officer rank. They were second-class citizens with all the obligations but none of the privileges in either the civilian or military sectors.[3]

From a long-range historical perspective, the strategy of accommodation to such discrimination was highly successful (we're still here), but one of the prices to be paid was the persistent attitude that Jews were reluctant to serve. Jews were indeed reluctant to serve in the militaries of countries with draconian draft laws, rampant discrimination, and the unlikelihood of promotion, especially to the officer class. However, in more tolerant countries, where opportunities existed, Jews were more than willing to serve. Their understandable avoidance of military service was repeatedly used as an instrument of oppression against them and resulted in the popular impression that Jews were unpatriotic.

---

2 Joseph W. Bendersky, *The Jewish Threat* (New York: Basic Books, 1990), 1–2.
3 Zvi Gitelman, "Why They Fought: What Soviet Jewish Soldiers Saw and How It Is Remembered," NCEER working paper (Seattle: University of Washington Press, 2011), 2.

This perception was far from the truth. In more tolerant countries, participation in the military was considered a viable path to social acceptance for some Diaspora Jews. The option of military service became more available to Jews during the Renaissance and the Enlightenment of the seventeenth and eighteenth centuries. As a result, Jews eagerly integrated themselves into these militaries whenever possible. When universal conscription was instituted in several European countries, many Jews sought the promise of equality. There they found great success, particularly in France, where Jews first were granted equality in most areas of life.

Universal conscription and admission to military schools were adopted as a matter of necessity by many European countries in the nineteenth century. The many wars fought by England, Germany, Austria-Hungary, Poland, Russia, and others required a steady stream of willing soldiers, among whom Jews were often disproportionately represented in an effort to be seen as worthy patriots.

It did not hurt that military participation was sanctioned by rabbis who encouraged their young men to go when hope for social integration was possible. One rabbi's sentiments best reflect this prevalent attitude in Jewish communities. He said, "If in combat you prove yourself to be an intrepid warrior, you show yourself to be a true Israeli; if after battle you behave like an upstanding Israelite, you prove as well that you are a true soldier."[4] When a country made real opportunity available, Jews took full advantage of it more times than not.

Unfortunately, these same countries and their militaries were often inconsistent in their relationship to Jews. Variances depended on the particular national leadership, the war, and the politics of the time. The length of a term of forced service could vary, limits were placed on the number of Jews allowed promotion within the officer corps, and the manner in which Jews were treated by peers was inconsistent and arbitrary.

---

4 Derek J. Penslar, *Jews and the Military* (Princeton, NJ: Princeton University Press, 2013), 140.

While Jews in general accounted for themselves extremely well in service, a stubborn, pervasive backdrop of anti-Semitism perpetuated a negative stereotype. In Europe at this time, many Jews who entered military service—either voluntarily, by draft, or by being impressed— were condescended to, and all too frequently their lives were made miserable.

Not until the establishment of the State of Israel in 1948 did Jews gain respect from the community of nations as courageous fighters, an image that stands today. Once the Jews had their country restored to them, the passive victim mentality was quickly transformed into an attitude that reflected Jewish enfranchisement. The new immigrants dropped Yiddish, the language of the ghetto, historical oppression, and the Holocaust, and Hebrew was revitalized, modernized, and made the new vernacular in the early twentieth century.

The stereotypical difference in attitudes between the Diaspora Jew and the Israeli Jew was exemplified during an episode of the TV prison drama *Oz* several years ago. A Russian Jewish immigrant is easily disposed of, much to the amazement of an inmate who states, "I thought Jews are supposed to be tough." "Only the Israelis," comes the knowing reply from the murderer. In the interest of survival, Jews are thankful that the stereotype of cowardly passivity stops at the Israeli border. However, the Diaspora Jew continues to live with the specter of physical inferiority and ethnic cowardice.

The irony in this vignette, which reflects a popular misconception, is that the line between Diaspora and Israeli Jews is anything but clearly defined. Moreover, the relative heroism and military competence of the Jew were not born overnight with the State of Israel. Rather these qualities are an extension of a military tradition that traces back to biblical times.

From the earliest centuries of the Diaspora through medieval times and up to the French Revolution and emancipation of the Jews, the Jewish soldier accounted for himself at least as well as his Gentile peers. Jews performed admirably on the battlefield for the country they happened to live in over the past two hundred years. The reality was that Israeli military success was not created in a vacuum. It was a product of their natural patriotic contributions, which they made during most of the two thousand years of the Diaspora.

In essence these experiences were the foundation of the military mindset necessary for success in the multiple wars that Israel has been forced to fight since 1948. Israel's military might was built directly on the backs of true warriors who developed their skills in conflicts in the late nineteenth and early twentieth centuries. They were veterans of revolution, resistance to anti-Semitic authority, civil wars, and, most importantly, World Wars I and II.

These collective combat experiences were instrumental to Israeli military success. They were a part of a long history of military participation that continues to the present day. The victory that is Israel is anything but an isolated historical event.

While Jewish children were generally discouraged from pursuing military careers in countries where anti-Semitism was fervent, the few who did often discovered that they had little hope of advancing too far in their chosen field if allowed to enter it at all. This critical factor, combined with the logical response of Jewish suspicion and abhorrence of the military in less tolerant countries, put intense pressure on Jewish children to use education as a means of social advancement. The de-emphasis of physicality in deference to intellectualism contributed to the military being among the least desirable of occupational options in Jewish homes.

Jewish parents had good reason to fear for their children who joined the military, whether by conscription or voluntarily. It would not be an unfair parallel to compare the Jewish military experience in certain European armies in less tolerant countries, such as Russia and Germany, to that of African Americans in the United States. In America it took an Act of Congress to rectify years of discrimination and neglect and honor the heroism of Jewish and other minority soldiers, marines, sailors, and airmen more than fifty years after their service.[5] While Jews were used because their numbers were needed, their efforts were often ignored, diminished, or denigrated. Jews, much like Blacks, often had to do better. A British Jewish veteran of World War II who was captured by the Germans told a fellow Jewish POW, "Because I'm Jewish I fight that much harder and because I'm Jewish I take greater risks to prove to other prisoners that Jewish people are as tough and resolute as any British POW or more so."[6] This double standard gradually subsided but it repeatedly reared its ugly head during World War II and the Korean War.

The Jewish War Veterans of the United States of America (JWV) was founded in 1896 as a direct reaction to a commonly held perception that *no* Jews served during the Civil War on either side. Two years earlier a Civil War Army officer was quoted in the influential *Harper's Weekly* that in his travels throughout the country he had never seen nor heard of any Jew who had served under the Union banner. This article marked the first time in American history that the old libel attacking Jewish patriotism had been circulated under such respectable auspices.[7] A second respected periodical, the *North American Review*, cited the Jews as unpatriotic parasites whose only participation in American wars was as camp followers, canteen merchants, or bounty hunters.[8] The reality was that about 6,000 to 8,000 Union and 2,000 to 3,000 Confederate Jewish soldiers served with distinction.[9] They were identified upon enlistment by their choice of chaplaincy, which dictated proper burial should they die in the service of their country. Unfortunately, in the minds of many, reality did not alter their basic perceptions, and just thirty years after the war ended, Jewish Civil War veterans were lost to history.

---

5 Donald H. Harrison, "Did Anti-Semitism Block Medals for Rocker's Namesake?" *San Diego Jewish Press-Heritage*, April 13, 2001.
6 Gitelman, "Why They Fought," 4.
7 Gloria Mosesson, *The Jewish War Veterans Story* (Washington, DC: Jewish War Veterans of the United States of America, 1971), 17.
8 Ibid.
9 Ibid., 16.

This stereotype flourished and was international in its scope well into the twentieth century. The Dreyfus Affair cited earlier, in which an honorable Jewish officer was falsely convicted by the French for spying for Germany and subsequently sent to Devil's Island for four years, cast suspicion on Jews in the French military in spite of their obvious contributions.

During World War I in Germany, more than 100,000 Jews fought for the kaiser. More than 12,000 were killed in action, and more than 35,000 received medals. (Perhaps the disproportionality compared to the entire population of Jews can be explained as an example of their need to prove themselves as "real Germans.") This phenomenon was repeated by Japanese Americans liberated from internment camps during World War II to fight for America against the Germans. One of their units ended the war with the highest casualty rate in the US Army (along with an inordinate number of medals). However, during the Nazi era, German Jewish battlefield achievements were dismissed to the degree that even Jewish World War I veterans who earned the Iron Cross were sent to the gas chambers. History was temporarily rewritten, and it was as if Jews never served.

While the American experience of military anti-Semitism in the twentieth century paled in comparison to that in Europe, many discriminatory episodes did occur. Two Jewish members of an eleven-man B-17 bomber crew were denied the medals their Gentile flight mates received because of the actions of an anti-Semitic captain (as Gen. Stan Newman told me). Gen. George S. Patton refused to allow Jewish chaplains in his Third Army.[10] A Jewish Korean War Army vet had to wait fifty years for his Medal of Honor.[11] The career of Admiral Hyman Rickover was mysteriously truncated under a cloud of anti-Semitism.[12] These are just a few of the incidents of

10 Leonard Dinnerstein, *Anti-Semitism in America* (New York: Oxford, 1994), 139.
11 See Wikipedia, s.v. "Tibor Rubin," https://en.wikipedia.org/wiki/Tibor_Rubin.
12 Robert Zubrin, "Rickover and the Nuclear Navy," *Fusion* 7, no. 4 (July–August 1985): 8–16.

anti-Semitism during World War II and the Korean War, which are thankfully rare in today's military.

Here is an interesting question. During World War II, who suffered more *combat* deaths, Jews (from all represented countries) or Americans? The correct answer is Americans (293,000) but by only a little over 30,000. The Jewish combat death total of approximately 260,000 is a figure that represents Jewish combat participation from at least eleven Allied countries and not just the United States.[13] The total would be even higher if Jewish partisan combat deaths were added.

The Cold War subsequently blinded most Americans, Jews and Gentiles alike, to Jews' overall contribution to the allied effort in World War II. Americans quickly forgot that the Soviet Union was a necessary ally against Nazi Germany, and the Jewish presence on the Eastern Front was forgotten as well, if it was ever appreciated at all.

While it is natural to dismiss one's current adversaries as formerly worthy brothers-in-arms because of historical shortsightedness, the reality was that the Soviet Army, which included 500,000 Jews, in Churchill's words, "Tore the guts out of the Wehrmacht."[14] Without these soldiers and the incredible sacrifices among them—approximately 200,000 Jewish dead—defeating the Nazis would have been that much more difficult. A rational, objective analysis of the contribution of Jews on the Eastern Front is entirely warranted. The fact that the majority of Jewish combat deaths were suffered by Soviet Jews does not diminish their significant role.

Who were these soldiers? They were representative of most Jews of the Diaspora, only they did not have the opportunity to leave the Soviet Union and its controlled territories partly because of restrictive US immigration policies after 1924. However, well over a million Jews served in the armies of the Western democracies. Again, with the "we try harder" motivation driving them, a disproportionate number

---

13 Gilbert, *Illustrated Atlas of Jewish Civilization*, 177.
14 Keith Cummins, *Cataclysm: The War on the Eastern Front* (Solihull: Helion & Co., 2011).

fought, died, and were decorated. Almost *half* of the Jews who served on the Eastern Front died in the fighting.[15] This is certainly a sacrifice worthy of note.

All this fighting and dying by the world's Jewry during World War II happened in the context of the worst period of anti-Semitism in American history. Leonard Dinnerstein, in his important work *Anti-Semitism in America* (1994), describes this particularly difficult time for Jews. It was a widely held belief that Jews not only didn't serve their country but that they were largely responsible for starting and perpetuating the war in the first place. The Jew in combat may have been given credit by the men they fought with, but these same men all too often considered him to be the exception and not the rule. In his book, Dinnerstein captures these attitudes with several examples of virulently anti-Semitic poems and parables popular at the time. One went as follows:

> The first American soldier to kill a Jap was Michael Murphy
> The first American bomber to sink a battleship was Captain Colin Kelly
> The first American to prove the effectiveness of a torpedo was Captain John Bulkley
> The first American flier to bag a Jap plane was John O'Hare
> The first American Coast Guardsman to detect a German spy was Ensign John Cullen
> The first American to be decorated by the President of the United States for bravery was Lieutenant Patrick Powers
> The first American to get new tires was Abe Cohen.[16]

Other documents in Dinnerstein's book are equally infuriating. They would lead one to believe that Jewish participation in the war was inconsequential and merely in a supportive capacity when Jews were in uniform (hence the Gregory Peck journalistic investigation in

---

15 Gilbert, *Illustrated Atlas of Jewish Civilization*, 177.
16 Dinnerstein, *Anti-Semitism in America*, 139.

Gentleman's Agreement). The truth is that in spite of cruel and prevalent anti-Semitism on both fronts, Jews not only were disproportionately represented in a favorable direction, they fought and died with distinction and without complaint wherever combat was taking place.

What could be more inspirational than to know there were no fewer than seventeen Medal of Honor recipients of Jewish origin? These men were awarded their commendations in every major American conflict and several minor ones. I quickly got out of the habit of sending Greg one hero per week because I felt that it was important to mention as many Jewish heroes as possible. More was definitely better, including three World War I veterans, one of whom appears at the end of the next letter.

07/12/2005

Dear Greg,

I have enjoyed researching Jewish military history and have forwarded an old book given to me by one of my uncles several years ago. It tells the story of the Jewish War Veterans organization and it is full of many surprising facts which I will relate to you in the proper context. Our history is even more impressive than I thought and is truly an international one that has had a significant impact on world events. Soon it will be your turn to be part of that history and you could not be in better company, from Abraham to Jack Jacobs and countless others in between. They all fought for what was right for their country but also for their people, and partly as a result we're still around.

```
    Next time I think I have a story about
Jewish isolation that you may or may not
have heard. It doesn't compare to your
ordeal but it may help a little. Until then,
continue to kick butt on those check rides!
                              Love, Norm
```

William Sawelson

William Sawelson was posthumously awarded the MOH for crawling to the aid of a wounded man while under fire. On his own initiative, Sgt. Sawelson left shelter and crawled through heavy machine-gun fire to bring his fellow combatant relief after the injured soldier began calling for water from a shell hole. Upon retrieving more water for the same soldier, Sgt. Sawelson was killed by machine-gun fire.

•

Greg loved the fact that one of his heroes, Gen. Hap Arnold, founder of the modern Air Force, was trained as a pilot by a Jewish immigrant. It certainly didn't hurt that Arnold has been credited with the distinction of introducing the scarf as an essential piece of pilot attire. Practically speaking, the scarf was worn outside the flight jacket and was used to wipe engine oil off the pilot's goggles. While the story of Arnold using his prayer shawl as his scarf and later being buried in it is colorful and dramatic, it is also entirely apocryphal.

```
                                    07/19/2005
Dear Greg,

It has been an extremely interesting histor-
ical search for these obscure Jews. Every
```

time I read about their accomplishments I get a little more proud and have more than enough ammunition to counter any allegation of Jewish nonparticipation.

These enlightening tidbits also speak loudly about Jewish isolation. Many of the Jewish heroes changed their names in an effort to reduce their visibility as Jews and assimilate more easily with their Christian peers. "Al Welsh" was one of them. What better tribute to a Jewish pilot than to have been Hap Arnold's instructor pilot?

Love, Norm

Laibel (Al) Wellcher

Born August 14, 1881, Al Welsh (né Wellcher), a test pilot for the Wright brothers, taught many aviation pioneers to fly, including Lt. Henry H. "Hap" Arnold, later a general and the Army's air chief of staff during World War II. According to legend, Al Welsh flew with a white scarf around his neck, a tradition that many of the early fliers who emulated him adopted after his death. Welsh later died in a crash.

•

My tenth letter represents the first time I ever spoke to Greg in greater detail about the Vietnam War and its impact on me. The subject is a sensitive one, but I thought it would be helpful at this stage of his career to understand the distinction I held between a war and its combatants. As history would have it, this distinction became useful, as the reader will see.

The exploits of the next luminary highlight Jewish heroism during the Vietnam War. Even though Jewish participation in this conflict was relatively low as opposed to that in other American wars, 150 Jews still died in combat, and several others—like John Levitow—distinguished themselves.

Air Force personnel rarely have the opportunity of being in a combat situation where earning a Medal of Honor is even possible. As a result I thought that a complete description of this enlisted airman's heroic acts would be particularly inspirational.

07/29/2005

Dear Greg,

It's exciting to hear about your progress in training. Also, you sound a lot more enthusiastic. Remember, it's all about the flying; all the rest is commentary.

Enclosed is [an account of] one of two Jewish Vietnam vets who was awarded the Medal of Honor. His is quite a story of heroism, and you can be especially proud because he was Air Force.

You know me well enough to know that Vietnam is a painful subject for me. I hated the war and its proponents for what it did to several friends of mine (including a Jewish combat vet) but I have managed to separate the war from the soldiers and airmen. It's odd but after all these years I still feel guilty that so many of my generation went and either died or suffered while I got out of it. For the record, I was drafted in 1969 and went for my physical, which I failed. I was assigned a 1-Y classification, i.e., to be called for duty in case of a national emergency. If I had passed I would have served. Deserting to Canada or Sweden was never an option. My guilt is not born of my failed patriotism but more because a part of me feels that I somehow let my peers down. They would never say so but it eats at me whenever the subject is brought up.

As a post-war baby boomer we were all brought up glorifying WWII and its participants, some of whom were inevitably relatives, like my three uncles. Vietnam was different and I didn't want to die for the cause but I would have for my buddies. Iraq has an eerie resemblance in many ways to Vietnam and again I am having to separate the war and its proponents from its combatants. When I think about your being in harm's way someday, it obviously pains me to think about your dying for little or nothing. However, I get considerable solace from knowing that fighting with and for your fellow airmen is most of what you will be doing. In this way, I feel in some small way that I am making up for my not sacrificing when my number was called. You can't pick your battles, you have to do as ordered, but you will also be doing it for your brothers in arms.

Maybe I'll get a commission and train the frontline crisis teams in emergency psychological interventions. Don't think

for a second that I wouldn't do this if
asked!! (Don't tell Carol.)

Love, Norm

John L. Levitow

For conspicuous gallantry and intrepidity in action at the risk of his own life above and beyond the call of duty, John L. Levitow (then airman first class), USAF, distinguished himself by exceptional heroism on February 24, 1969, while assigned as a loadmaster aboard an AC-47 flying a night mission. On that date, Levitow's was struck by a hostile mortar round while launching flares to provide illumination for army ground troops engaged in combat. The resulting explosion ripped a hole through the wing, and fragments made over 3,500 holes in the fuselage. The explosion also tore the cargo compartment open, and the crew was helplessly slammed against the floor. Levitow, though stunned by the concussion of the blast and suffering from over forty fragment wounds in his back and legs, staggered to his feet and turned to assist the man nearest to him, who had been knocked away from the open cargo compartment door. Then Levitow saw the smoking flare ahead of him in the aisle. Realizing the danger involved and completely disregarding his own wounds, Levitow smothered the flare with his hands as much as possible and threw himself bodily upon it. Hugging the deadly device to his body, he dragged himself back to the rear of the aircraft and hurled the flare through the open cargo door. At that instant, the flare separated and ignited in the air, but clear of the aircraft.

Levitow, by his selfless and heroic actions, saved the aircraft and its entire crew from certain destruction and death. His profound concern for his fellow men and his intrepidity at the risk of his own life above and beyond the call of duty are in keeping with the highest traditions of the USAF and reflect great credit upon himself and the armed forces of his country.

•

In my next letter to Greg I offered the hypothetical scenario described prior to the fall of the Alamo, which I thought would be interesting for him to contemplate. The Talmud wrestles with such subjects, and I considered that the Wolf story, however apocryphal it might be, would be particularly relevant. The idea of a Jew being at the Alamo should not have been surprising to Greg or anyone else. My cousin Byron Price, former director of the University of Oklahoma Press and Western art history professor at OU, is the Byron I refer to in the letter.

08/03/2005

Dear Greg,

Researching Jewish military history has been fun for me and no effort at all. It lets me know more about why Byron is so passionate about his work. For me as an amateur historian and professional Jew, it reveals the true international experiences of our people who show up in the strangest of places.

There were allegedly three Jews who died at the Alamo, Avram Wolf and his two sons. What I found to be fascinating was the fact that a 4th Jew, Louis Rose, left during a brief amnesty 3 days before the final assault which killed the Wolfs.

There is no way to really know the motives of these two men but it is interesting to speculate on what transpired before they made their fateful decisions. Did they talk to each other, and if they did, was each one's Jewishness a factor? Wolf stayed for a cause that cost the lives of his sons. Did they (the boys) stay on their own and against his will? Did Rose leave for the sake of his family and should Wolf have done the same? These are questions worthy of the Talmud, one of the most important of which is the one dealing with family and country (or cause).

Love, Norm

Avram Wolf

Avram Wolf, a widower from England, was accompanied to the Alamo by his two young sons, Michael and Benjamin, ages twelve and eleven, respectively. All three were killed in the defense of Texas. Since the Mexicans offered amnesty to any Alamo defender who wished to surrender a few days before the final battle, the question arises as to why the boys were present at the end. Rather than speculate, it is best to consider all three heroes and let them rest in peace and honor.

CHAPTER 4

The Responsibility of a Jew

"The responsibility of a Jew is *tikkun olam*, to repair a broken world."

—Jewish proverb

AFTER LEARNING ABOUT JEWISH MILITARY HEROES across history, I thought it would be helpful to Greg to find a person alive at the time to serve as a role model. I began the search by locating an expert in Jewish military history who told me about a book he had written about various Jewish military figures. At this point I was simply hoping for a Jewish pilot with some combat experience. The person I found exceeded all my wildest expectations. His name is Stan Newman.

Gen. Newman is a two-star general who flew with distinction in World War II. On a whim I cold-called him and wrote to him about Greg's military service and experiences. To my surprise and delight,

Stan Newman in his F-86 Sabre jet.

Gen. Newman was not only forthcoming with information, he attended Greg's wing ceremony at Vance Air Force Base (AFB).

Gen. Newman was very interested in Greg's progress as a pilot and later in combat. The general had an incredible career as a highly decorated combat pilot in World War II, Korea, and Vietnam. His awards include the Distinguished Service Medal, Legion of Merit, two Distinguished Flying Crosses, Meritorious Service Medal, and fourteen Air Medals. Gen. Newman is a treasure trove of information to this very day. We trade books, speak occasionally on the phone, and send notes back and forth. I've never been so rewarded from acting on a whim.

In 2013, Gen. Newman was presented the medal of Chevalier (Knight) of the French National Order of the Legion of Honour. The award was established by Napoleon Bonaparte in 1802 and is France's highest decoration. It was awarded to Gen. Newman because he took part in the liberation of France during World War II. He flew air

Retired Maj. Gen. Stanley Newman receives the Medal of Chevalier of the French National Order of the Legion of Honour from Grant Moak, honorary French consul for Oklahoma, March 16, 2013.

support for the French 1st Army as well as American units during their push into Germany. In this capacity he was credited with two air victories, the second of which represented one of the last German fighters downed in the war in May 1945. Gen. Newman strongly identified as a Jew. During one of our many conversations he told me of his fears of being shot down over Germany. It was not so much death he feared but that no one would be there to say Kaddish, the Jewish mourning prayer, for him. Greg finally had as exemplar a living, highly decorated Jewish fighter pilot who used his faith in times of adversity. I couldn't have asked for more. It was without reservation that I dedicated this book to him.

At Greg's wings ceremony, Gen. Newman presented a compilation of World War II stories (titled *Tails to Tales*) of the 185th Fighter Squadron of which he was a part. "Check six" is a reminder to Greg to be vigilant about who might be on his tail.

•

I had been scanning through a list of Jewish pilots at the Battle of Britain (about thirty of them), which included brief excerpts from their combat experiences. Suddenly I came upon an obscure pilot whose incredible résumé included one air victory after another as well as a series of harrowing, death-defying incidents, all of which could only impress the most experienced of pilots.

What made this pilot's achievements so significant in the context of my letters to Greg is that they occurred during the most crucial air battle in history. The time was the summer of 1940, when Great Britain stood alone against the mighty Nazi war machine. Hitler had conquered almost all of Europe from the Atlantic Ocean to the border of the Soviet Union, and he was now prepared to administer the final blow to a reeling Great Britain with a full-scale invasion.

First, he had to establish air superiority, which would allow the invasion to take place much more easily, and this is where the heroic battle begins. This time was particularly relevant to the Jews because if a successful invasion and occupation of Great Britain had been achieved, the war would have gone on indefinitely and Hitler would have had more time to effect his Final Solution.

As it was, six of the nine million European Jews were murdered in the course of the war. Countless more would have certainly been slaughtered if the Allies had been forced to take back Great Britain before mounting an invasion of the continent. An undertaking of this magnitude would have taken a lot of time, something European Jews had little of under the best circumstances.

From the most authoritative accounts, Flt. Lt. Tuck was one of six hundred or so Royal Air Force (RAF) pilots available to meet the seemingly endless waves of German warplanes that came at England on a daily basis for about four months. Fortunately for the free world the determination, tenacity, and skill of these RAF heroes thwarted every incursion, and Germany was forced to delay its invasion indefinitely. This modest lieutenant was one of the RAF heroes.

It takes five air victories to qualify for "ace" status. Lt. Tuck shot down thirty (he claims thirty-five) Nazi warplanes, making him a *sextuple* ace. If his air-to-air combat skills weren't enough, his appearance completed the picture of the quintessential fighter pilot. I was hoping for someone who fit the part, and when I found his picture I could not have been more gratified. Here was a pilot who looked like a combination of Errol Flynn and David Niven and carried himself with a supreme air of confidence and a bit of a swagger, the way any true fighter pilot should.

When one throws in such facts as his surviving four crashes, two midair collisions, internment in a POW camp, and an escape from a POW camp, and finally finishing the war as a line officer with the Russians, the man becomes that much more legendary. He was the perfect role model, and he served Greg well during his journey.

Flt. Lt. Tuck certainly should be included as one of Judaism's greatest warriors, along with Judah Maccabee and Bar Kochba, a Jewish military leader who led the Bar Kokhba revolt against the Roman Empire in 132 CE. It is unfortunate that Jews, or anyone else for that matter, don't know more about him. Perhaps someday he will get his due, but until then I am comforted from knowing that one of his spiritual descendants has benefited from his influence to accomplish extraordinary things.

An entry in Tuck's flight log, which I gave to Greg at his wings ceremony, sums up the best of Flt. Lt. Tuck. It simply reads, "Jumped by 3 ME-109s, shot down 2 and damaged the third." Fearless, efficient, and deadly—enough said.

08/10/2005

Dear Greg,

Prepare to "meet" who is most certainly the greatest Jewish fighter pilot in history, Flt. Lt. Robert Tuck. What a story! What

makes guys like him even more impressive
is the fact that even in Britain it was
extremely hard for Jews to break into the
officer corps. Tuck was one of many Jewish
pilots from numerous countries who helped
turn the tide of WWII.

I'll be sending you more about the Jewish
pilots like Tuck who did their share. They
are true heroes whose contributions no one
can remove from history of which you are
now a part.

Love, Norm

Robert Stanford Tuck

As a flight commander over Dunkirk on May 23, 1940, in his
Spitfire, he shot down three 110s and a 109; on May 24, two
Do 17s; on May 25, shared (i.e., shot down in conjunction with
another pilot) a Do 17; on June 2, a 109 and He 111, and two 109s
damaged. He was wounded in this incident. His squadron leader
at the time was Roger Bushell, of *The Great Escape* fame and whom
he later met again at the Sagan POW camp after capture. When
Bushell was shot down over Dunkirk, Tuck took over as squadron
leader. Tuck was awarded the Distinguished Flying Cross (DFC)
for "initiative and personal example over Dunkirk" on June 11,
1940, and received it on June 28 from King George VI at a special
ceremony at Hornchurch.

He continued shooting the enemy out of the sky—shared a Do 17
on July 8, damaged a Ju 88 on July 25, shared a Ju 88 on August 13,
destroyed two Ju 88s on August 14 and two on August 18, but he was
shot down that day, bailing out with an injury over Horsmonden (his

Spitfire crashing at Tucks Cottage, Park Farm) on the estate of Lord Cornwallis—who then invited him to tea!

On August 25 he shot down another Do 17, but his plane was shot up and he glided fifteen miles to the coast with a dead engine off St. Gowan's Head and crash landed. On September 11, commanding 257 Squadron, he shot down a 110 and 109; on September 23, a 109; on October 4, a Ju 88; on October 12, a 109; on October 25, a 109 and two damaged; and on October 28, two more 109s! He was awarded a bar to the DFC on October 25, 1940, with the *Times* writing, "In the face of constant death he preserved a lightness of heart which was not simply bravura but allied to precise and ruthlessly applied technical skill." On December 19, now flying Hurricanes, he shot down another Do 17; on December 12, a 109; on December 29, a Do 17. He was awarded the Distinguished Service Order (DSO) on January 7, 1941, "for leading 257 Squadron with great success. . . . His outstanding leadership, courage and skill have been reflected in its high morale and efficiency." The king awarded the DSO and announced the second bar to Tuck on January 28, 1941, and at the same ceremony awarded the DFC to his good friend Brian van Mentz (see below): a unique occasion for two Jewish RAF officers to be decorated together.

Tuck continued. March 2 and 19, 1941, two more Do 17s; April 9, a Ju 88; April 27, damaged a Ju 88; and May 11 shot down two more Ju 88s. He received his second bar to the DFC on April 11, 1941, "for conspicuous gallantry and initiative in searching for and attacking enemy raiders, often in adverse weather conditions"; he was only the second RAF pilot to win such a distinction.

On June 21, 1941, he destroyed two 109s and damaged another but was himself wounded and shot down in the English Channel— but then picked up in his dinghy by a Gravesend coal barge after two hours. As wing leader at Duxford commanding three squadrons, he shot down three more 109s. He was then sent as a liaison officer to the United States with other aces, including "Sailor" Malan, and then returned to Biggin Hill as a wing leader. On January 28, 1942, he was shot down by flak on a low-level strafing attack outside Boulogne and made a POW. He was interviewed by Adolf Galland and after the war—ironically for a Jewish pilot—made an honorary member of Galland's old German squadron.

In various camps, he helped plan the "great escape" from Sagan but was moved before the breakout. He finally escaped on February 1, 1945, with Flt. Lt. Zbigniew Kustrzynski and met up with the Russians and spent two weeks fighting with them. They then made their way to the British Embassy in Moscow and were sent to Southampton by ship via Odessa. Tuck was awarded the US Distinguished Flying Cross on June 14, 1946.

Tuck was shot down four times, collided twice, was wounded twice, bailed out, crash landed, and was dunked in the Channel! Volume 1 of the *Official History of the Royal Air Force* states, "They had that restless spirit of aggression, that passion to be at grips with the enemy, which is the hallmark of the very finest troops. Some—like Bader, Malan and Stanford Tuck—were so fiercely possessed of this demon, and of the skill to survive the danger into which it drew them, that their names were quickly added to the immortal company of Ball, Bishop, Mannock and McCudden."

Tuck is probably the most highly decorated Jewish World War II pilot after Arthur Louis Aaron, VC, DFM. Tuck is credited with thirty kills—one not added until 1982—making him the eighth-ranking ace of the RAF, with more victories than any other *British* pilot. His portrait hangs at Bentley Priory RAF base at Stanmore—Fighter Command headquarters in World War II—alongside those of many other Battle of Britain pilots. He died at age seventy on May 5, 1987.

•

Three years after this next letter was written I discovered a book titled *The Few* that was about the original eight members of the Eagle Squadron. (The Eagle Squadron comprised three fighter squadrons that were formed prior to entry into WWII.) I gave it to Greg. "The Mad Russian" Mamedoff is credited with being the first Jewish American pilot to fly in combat against the Nazis.

The other reference in the letter is to Sgt. Stephen Austin Levenson, who was shot down during the Battle of Britain. Seeing Greg's last name in the scroll of these heroes was both uplifting and saddening at the same time—and a little creepy.

08/16/2005

Dear Greg,

As best I can tell Mamedoff was the only Jewish pilot in the Eagle Squadron which consisted of dozens of American airmen who wanted into the fight two years before the US got involved. God bless them partially because sentiment against the war was so strong at the time. "Andy," like you, tried to get in two times before he was accepted. Anti-Semitism may have been a factor in his rejections especially by the French. Regarding the other guy, it is awesome to see Levenson in the list of Jewish RAF pilots. It sort of brings history to life and makes it more cohesive.

Love, Norm

Andrew (Andy) B. Mamedoff

Andrew B. Mamedoff was a pilot officer from the United States with 609 Squadron. An American researcher has confirmed with AJEX (the Association of Jewish Ex-Servicemen and Women) that he was

Jewish, son of Natalie and husband of Alys (née Craven) of London. He was born August 24, 1912, and brought up in Thompson, Connecticut. He performed in air shows and at the outbreak of the war tried to fight with the Finnish Air Force and later the French Air Force but failed. Mamedoff had to stow away to the United Kingdom, where he was given an emergency commission in the RAF and sent to a Spitfire squadron on August 8, 1940, with two other Americans he had met in France. They became the first three members of the Eagle Squadron, which eventually comprised 244 American volunteers who fought throughout the battle. On a flight to a posting to Northern Ireland on October 8, 1941, he failed to arrive, and his body was later recovered for burial at Brookwood Cemetery, grave 21.A.7.

•

I again returned to the Vietnam War, a time of perceived Jewish military underrepresentation. Increasingly, Greg had been bothered by his Jewish peers' apathetic attitude about military service as well as their lack of appreciation for what he was striving to do. While he understood the historical antecedents of this phenomenon, it irked him nevertheless.

Although Greg thought that he was the only Jew on a base of over nine hundred airmen at Vance AFB, Enid, Oklahoma, the vice commander of the base, Col. Jerry Siegal, was Jewish. At the celebration after the wings ceremony at Vance, Greg pointed out Col. Siegal. Not being the shy sort, I went over to him, introduced myself, and asked if he were Jewish. He quickly replied, "With a schnozz like this, what else could I be?"

09/19/2005

Dear Greg,

Here is a real oddity, a Vietnam-era Jewish
fighter pilot who distinguished himself at

a time when many Jews, like myself, were doing everything possible to avoid the war. I would be interested in learning more about guys like him. I'm convinced that some people are born warriors in the sense that other people are born to do other things. That is, they are destined to serve in the armed forces regardless of family pressure, peer influence, or political circumstance.

During Vietnam, while many Jews served, many others didn't for the same reason their Gentile counterparts didn't, i.e., their belief in the injustice of the war. Unwittingly they perpetuated the myth of the Jewish coward. I can assure you that if the war were more "legitimate," Jews would have served like everyone else, including myself, but Vietnam was a different story. Your peers' resistance to serving may, in part, be an extension of that attitude. I hope that there is never a war in which Jews can again prove themselves but if there is you definitely won't be so alone.

You were born to fly and to be a warrior. It's almost like you don't have a choice and people without that passion can't identify at all. I feel comforted each time I meet a fellow warrior, not so much for the sake of our country, but for your sake.

As you know 18 is the luckiest number in Kabalistic numerology. If I remember correctly you had 18 in your officer candidate class and it looks like you will have

```
18 in your graduating flight class. Does
this tell you something? Probably not, but
get an 18 somewhere on your Viper (F-16)
just in case.
                                   Love, Norm
```

Fred Zedeck

After earning his navigator's wings in 1969, Capt. Fred Zedeck completed his flight training and was certified as an Air Force navigator/weapons systems officer who flew as a back-seater on the F-4 Phantom. In the Southeast Asia area of operations during the Vietnam War, Capt. Zedeck served with the 388th Tactical Fighter Wing in Korat, Thailand. There he flew 165 combat missions and logged more than 450 combat hours. Of the many decorations he earned, two were the Air Force Distinguished Flying Cross (fourth-highest combat award) and the Air Medal with Ten Oak Leaf Clusters.

•

I thought it was important to provide a list of Jewish war heroes that included as many American conflicts as possible. This letter pointed out that Jews were actively involved in military events of historical import.

09/23/2005

```
Dear Greg,

I know that you enjoy the pilots' histories
better, but for a full historical apprecia-
tion of your fellow brothers-in-arms I have
included the following. These additions
```

prove complete Jewish participation in
every single major conflict the US has
been in since the Revolutionary War. Now if
you run across some asshole who questions
Jewish patriotism and combat participation
you can pull a name from any conflict. To
all of these Jewish vets, a job well done
and may they all rest in eternal peace.

Love, Norm

North Carolina's Alfred Mordecai was raised to the rank of major for meritorious service in the line of duty during the Mexican War, 1846–1848.

When the USS *Maine* was sunk in Havana on February 15, 1898, fifteen Jewish sailors perished along with their Christian brothers. The ship's executive officer was Adolph Marix, who became a vice admiral in the navy.

During the Spanish–American War, the first Rough Rider to die in combat was Jacob Wilbusky, a sixteen-year-old boy.

CHAPTER 5

The Tears of a Woman

"God counts the tears of a woman."

—Jewish meditation

CAROL'S AND MY PARENTING PHILOSOPHY WAS deceptively simple: trade freedom for responsibility. As long as Greg made his grades, did what we asked around the house, and was respectful, he got what he wanted. Of course, it always helps keep domestic life in balance if the kid has an abiding passion. In Greg's case, it was flight.

Greg was by no means a "perfect" child, but in reality he was easy to raise. He earned a hardship driver's license three weeks after his fifteenth birthday and qualified for a pilot's license at seventeen. I mostly stopped worrying about him at this point. I vividly remember him sitting in front of the TV watching preflight videos and studying pilot manuals for countless hours and still tending to his other responsibilities.

The Federal Aviation Administration (FAA) has no tolerance for carelessness. Greg well knew that any lapse in judgment, such as drinking too close to flight time, would cost him dearly. He made most of his childhood easy for us and carried his good habits into adulthood.

Jewish women, like their male counterparts, have been well represented in the military. In the Reform movement women are allowed to serve as rabbis and *sofrot* (scribes), and of course serve their countries in the military. In Israel, it is even mandatory for women to serve—and serve they do, making up 69 percent of all positions.

The women I've known would have an especially important role in the Texas stages of my life. Shortly after moving from Concord to Houston in 1988, I began developing mysterious urological symptoms. Without warning I would have episodic bladder spasms that were quite disruptive to my busy life. For seventeen years, I struggled with symptoms and saw various specialists who could not identify the problem. I was even told by a kidney specialist in Arkansas that it was "all in your head."

Finally, in 2006, I was diagnosed by a urologist at MD Anderson Cancer Center in Houston with grade 3 urethral cancer, a very rare and deadly form of the disease. I would endure two months of taxing chemotherapy, and then I would have radical genitourinary surgery. My oncologist pulled no punches and said there was a 50 to 70 percent chance of survival if every phase of treatment went as planned.

During recovery, I had lost a total of forty-seven pounds. Once after a rehab session to regain my strength, I fell on the floor and told God I was ready to go. At that moment, I realized that there are some things worse than death. My disease, treatment, and recovery are things I wouldn't wish upon anyone. However, because of Carol's unfailing love, devotion, and attentiveness, along with family and friends who sat with her and helped her during the long days at MD Anderson, we overcame, together. It took a village to recover, so during my long rehabilitation I welcomed the support of a small Baptist church in Silverton, Texas, which had been alerted by my mother-in-law as to my plight. Their congregation, comprising people I never met, unfailingly sent me weekly prayer cards, which touched me deeply.

Greg visited me in Houston during the worst of my treatment. At that time, we had "the talk" about my mortality, our relationship, and my postmortem wishes. He handled all of this as well as possible. I was not to worry about my illness affecting his concentration in the air. Not without considerable struggle, he graduated and moved on to the F-16 as I was showing signs of improvement.

I found myself increasingly applying to myself the inspiration from the Jewish military figures in the letters I sent to Greg. In retrospect, when I felt down and out, I started reflecting on how these characters used their faith to surmount the obstacles they faced. If they could do it, Greg and I could too, and we did. One such inspiring figure was Lydia Litvyak, who volunteered for the Russians. Lydia, a Russian Jew, was an awesome combat pilot who shot down twelve Nazi warplanes as part of an all-female combat fighter group. Second Lt. Frances Slanger, an Army nurse, was killed by German artillery while she was tending to American soldiers shortly after D-Day. At that time the only women allowed near the front line were nurses.

On a more personal note, significant support during my struggle with cancer came from a totally unexpected source: a brave woman afflicted with the same cancer I had. A neighbor of ours realized one day that a friend and coworker of hers was my diagnostic cohort. This urethral cancer group consisted of myself and three women who for obvious reasons were unable to realize that something was very wrong as early as I was.

My neighbor's friend, Beverly K., was having difficulty coping with our grim prognoses partly because she was hearing comments from her religiously fundamentalist friends that were far from helpful. In fact, they were adding to her sense of hopelessness and despair.

My neighbor must have sensed that I could offer Beverly something her co-religionists could not and suggested that Beverly talk to me about it, which she did. It turns out that she was hearing things like, "Accept this, it is God's will" and "You'll be in a better place," which she found to be not only unsupportive but worsening her outlook and thus her chances of recovery.

I was able to give Beverly the support she needed without the negativity and suggested she use God for support and not as a source for self-denigration, guilt, and helplessness. It was much more comforting to her to view God in a loving manner. From this conversation evolved a true friendship born of mutual fear, suffering, and empathy.

I only met Beverly once. We both happened to be at MD Anderson at the same time in various stages of treatment. One day she very unexpectedly came to visit, along with her IV pole, and it was great to put a kind face to her voice. She seemed at peace with her spiritual dilemma. After a brief visit, Carol walked her back to her room. I never saw her again, and she died shortly thereafter.

•

There was much more to be said for Germany's Jewish fighter pilots of World War I who spoke to the ethnic isolation issue better than any other group. They fought not only the enemy but their fellow officers and even enlisted personnel as well. They deserve the utmost respect in spite of the side they fought on.

Here I also made my first pitch for a call name with Jewish historical significance. This came to pass, but not in the way I thought it would.

08/19/2005

Dear Greg,

Talk about fighting religious discrimination and succeeding! There were 130 Jewish fighter pilots flying for Germany during WWI. Sounds like a lot to me. It's hard to imagine what these guys went through. One of the saddest chapters in Jewish history is what happened to all these WWI heroes after the Nazis came to power. They were not only stripped of their medals and essentially (if temporarily) written out of German history, but they were stripped of their lives as well. If my memory serves me correctly, they were the last of the German Jews to be murdered, Hitler's only concession to their service to the Fatherland.

Moral of the story—when some asshole imparts anti-Semitism toward you, put it all in perspective and remain indifferent. When you fly, in a sense you fly for Frankl and every other Jewish pilot or frustrated pilot denied their destiny or place in history due to prejudice.

I can't wait to talk to you in person about this material. Two weeks to go. Fly well and on the tails of these great men who preceded you until then.

Love, Norm

P.S. A friend of mine, well-versed in military history, had heard of "Lucky Tuck" but didn't know he was Jewish. How about "Tuck" for a call name? I'll never give up hoping that your call name has a Jewish twist.

Wilhelm Frankl

Wilhelm Frankl is the best-known German Jewish fighter pilot of World War I. He was born in Hamburg on December 20, 1893, and his family later moved to Frankfurt am Main. After graduating from school, Frankl went to Germany's famous aviation center at Johannisthal and took flying lessons from Germany's first female pilot, Melli Beese. After the war started, he volunteered for the air service and proved to be an outstanding fighter pilot. In 1916 Frankl became engaged to the Christian daughter of an Austrian naval officer, and he made a controversial decision to convert to Christianity. Some say he converted to please his future wife, while others maintain he converted in the hope that he would have better career opportunities. (Jews in Germany were not allowed the same rights as Christians.)

In a short amount of time Frankl shot down several enemy planes, and soon afterward his picture was featured on German postcards and he was hailed as a national hero. Frankl received the Pour le Mérite (nicknamed the "Blue Max"), which was Germany's equivalent to America's Medal of Honor. He was made commander of his own squadron, Jasta 4.

Frankl was killed on April 8, 1917, when the Albatross D.III he was flying fell apart during combat over France. Just three days before he had shot down three enemy aircraft in one day, for a total of nineteen. He was buried in Berlin–Charlottenburg, but his grave has been lost to war and history. Frankl was excluded from *Pour le mérite-Flieger*, Walter Zuerl's 1938 chronicle of German World War I fighter pilots who had received the award. In spite of his conversion, Frankl apparently was, in Nazi eyes, still a Jew. A Jew was defined as someone who had at least one Jewish grandparent.

In 1973, the West German Luftwaffe named a squadron after him.

•

Over one hundred Jews served in America's first war as a sovereign nation. This next hero's Hispanic name derives from his being a descendant of the Jews who were forcibly expelled from Spain in the fifteenth century. The Jews of Spanish, Portuguese, and North

African origin are called "Sephardic," which means "Spanish" in Yiddish.

Knowing Jewish history, Salvador would have relished the idea of fighting for a country that wanted him and his fellow Jews and allowed them to practice their faith in peace. His fight, as it has been for many Jews since the birth of the United States, was as much for his people as it was for his country.

08/23/2005

```
Dear Greg,


I thought I would change things up a little
and get back to Earth with Francis Salvador.
In spite of what this says about having the
dubious honor of being the first Jew to die
for his country, I consider his death to be
anything but dubious. He died for something
vital and his efforts are well supported
by Jewish teachings. From my best count
about 15,000 Jews died for the US in all
wars including "minor" conflicts, as you
will see in later letters. They believed in
whatever cause they were fighting for and
they were just as courageous and sacrific-
ing as any of their Christian counterparts.
                              Love, Norm
```

Francis Salvador

After being elected the first Jewish delegate to South Carolina's revolutionary Provincial Congress in 1774, Francis Salvador became a strong proponent of American independence.

On July 1, 1776, just three days before the ratification of the Declaration of Independence, Salvador rode thirty miles to warn South Carolinian settlers of the threat from Cherokees who had allied themselves with the British. Later he returned to the front lines to join the militiamen who were defending settlements under siege.

On August 1, 1776, during a Cherokee attack, Salvador was shot and killed. The Jewish Paul Revere was the first of his people to die for the cause of American freedom.

•

In the next letter, my cousin Byron Price is referred to once again. Byron is a West Point graduate and a real historian (unlike me), a much-published author of Western history and Western art history texts. When Greg earned his wings, Byron presented Greg with his West Point sword. When asked why he was giving such a prized possession away, he responded, "I'm not giving it away. I'm giving it to Greg."

08/30/2005

Dear Greg,

Welcome home!

Even though you won't get these through the mail, I didn't want a week to pass without your distinguished military figures and related issues.

I wonder how Simon Levy was treated. Imagine, a Jew in the very first West Point class. Byron will be proud about my historical research. How ironic it is for you to have to use your faith as strength to cope

```
with fellow airmen. I'm sure you are up to
this challenge as you've been with all the
others they threw at you.
   Keep it up. Lt. Tuck and all the others
who came before you and had to handle the
same horseshit would be proud.
                              Love, Norm
```

Simon M. Levy

Simon M. Levy from Baltimore, Maryland, was the first Jew to be appointed a cadet, in the very first class at West Point Military Academy in 1802. Since then, more than nine hundred Jews have graduated from the Academy.

Uriah P. Levy

The first Jewish American commodore in the US Navy was Uriah P. Levy. He served with distinction in the War of 1812 and was instrumental in abolishing corporal punishment in the Navy. He experienced much anti-Semitism during his service and, as a consequence reflective of the time, had to fight many duels. Many of those serving with him thought that, as a Jew, he was unfit to hold such a high rank. Commodore Levy ended the War of 1812 as the highest-ranking US naval officer.

•

The following "Jewku" (a play on the Japanese haiku) apparently amused Greg enough to include in his Air Force catalogue, a composite scrapbook of all his training experiences. A poet I'm not, but I was flattered nonetheless to be featured in his documentation.

September 6, 2005

Dear Greg,

A "Jewku" for your thoughts . . .

> While you will fly a single-seat fighter
> You will never be alone
> For you will fly with every great
> Jewish pilot
> Who preceded you
> And for every child deprived of the
> dream of flight
> Solely because he was born a Jew.

Love, Norm

•

My favorite discovery among the reams of material available on Jewish military history was the multinational Jewish participation at the Battle of Britain. Jews came from around the world to fight against Nazism—from the United States, Canada, Palestine, South Africa, India, and Poland. Not only were they heroic figures, they were real characters in the humorous sense of the word as well. For example, one irreverent and rebellious Polish pilot refused a direct order against engaging a German airplane in dense fog. He took a plane, without permission, shot the German down, and then reported to his supervisor for consequences. He was allowed to continue fighting.

These men were all volunteers who traveled great distances to be part of the action. What was going on in occupied Europe against the Jews could have been a factor, or maybe they were just looking for a good fight. The fact was that they were there as perhaps unwitting representatives of the Jewish people, and they accounted for themselves extremely well.

09/07/2005

Dear Greg,

I couldn't resist sending you the names of these three Jewish airmen who flew in the Battle of Britain. The fact that makes them interesting is that while they are all Jews they are from three different countries. They all heard the call, traveled long distances voluntarily, and fought bravely. Their countries of origin are proof of the Diaspora and their coming together is proof of the solidarity of the Jewish people. As officer Nelson stated, "I thank God that I shall be able to help to destroy the regime that persecutes the Jews." He and the others were yet another testament against the widely held perception that Jews went like sheep to the slaughter.

I especially like the little stories that make these men come alive. I was only kidding you the other day when I asked under what conditions you could refuse an order from a superior officer. Sgt. Pilot Ziggy Klein actually did what was in keeping with an aspect of Jewish character because his hatred for the Germans overrode any concern for consequences. He was so overcome with what was happening to Jews in Poland that he refused a direct order not to fly on a day that had abysmal flying conditions in order to shoot down a German plane. He did so and landed, fully prepared to accept the consequences of his actions.

Van Mentz was killed by a bomb after drinking with none other than Lt. Tuck (lucky yet again) after living through 75 sorties and bagging several German planes. And of course Nelson's taking on six 109s singlehandedly speaks for itself.

Of course, most of the names from this battle were KIA or MIA because they had to fly so frequently and they wouldn't have it any other way. It is very sad but it is an incredibly proud chapter in Jewish military history.

Love, Norm

Distinguished in the Battle of Britain

Lt. William Nelson, Canadian Jewish fighter pilot
Sgt. Ziggy Klein, Polish Jewish fighter pilot
Lt. Brian van Mentz, British Jewish fighter pilot
—all of whom distinguished themselves during the crucial Battle of Britain.

•

Greg flew into his hometown of Lubbock, Texas, on a cross-country training exercise. Following a brief visit, he performed the classic wing-tipping maneuver after takeoff for the benefit of his family below. He was beginning to gain more confidence, but I wanted to keep him humble by pointing out who defined confidence in this case: Lt. Tuck and his RAF mates. In the letter I refer to the Tacos—the call name for the 150th Fighter Squadron of the New Mexico Air National Guard. Greg joined the Tacos at the completion of his undergraduate pilot, intermediate fighter, and advanced fighter training.

09/12/2005

Dear Greg,

Talk about isolation—Sam Grass found himself in Haiti fighting in some Godforsaken war against the Caco bandits—whoever they were. Very dramatic stuff. He is another Jew who felt compelled to change his name. My mother's maiden name is a derivation (Margolis) of Margulies meaning that the families resided reasonably close to each other in Russian-occupied Poland where most of us come from.

I can't tell you how much it meant to me (us) to see you last week. The wing-tipping was over the top and we swelled with pride. However, these experiences will definitely give you a mental edge in the long run in much the same way that the Israelis have a definite psychological advantage over their adversaries.

I hope all is well—I can see your confidence growing, which is of great comfort.

Love, Norm

Sam Gross

On November 17, 1915, as part of a detachment of sailors and Marines, Sam Gross attacked the old French bastion at Fort Rivière, Haiti, to cut off the rebelling bandits' retreat. Gross was the second man to pass through a breach in the wall in the face of constant fire. Thereafter, for ten minutes, he engaged the enemy in desperate hand-to-hand combat until the fort was captured and Caco resistance was neutralized.

•

The exceptional soldier reported on next was liberated from a concentration camp in 1945 by US troops when he was a teenager. Upon seeing American soldiers, he became awestruck with them and their uniforms and vowed to become a soldier himself, partly in acknowledgment to his rescuers and their country. A few years after he emigrated to the United States, the Korean War started and he enlisted. He earned the Medal of Honor. Unfortunately, it took fifty-five years for him to receive his medal, at least partly because of persistent anti-Semitic attitudes in the military that conspired to block discovery of his accomplishments. He expressed no bitterness or resentment at the delay but rather accepted his medal with pride, grace, and gratitude.

"Track select" in the letter refers to the point in training when the pilot candidate discovers what advanced aircraft he or she will be assigned. Greg was only one out of the four out of twenty-six in his class who were assigned to a fighter. He qualified for F-16 training.

09/26/2005

Dear Greg,

Since it is track-select week I thought that you deserved two interesting stories.

I got so caught up on Congressional Medal of Honor winners to the point that I had overlooked all the other Jewish servicemen who performed above and beyond, like Sgt. Tibor Rubin. Rubin's story is fascinating because of its uniqueness. I can assure you that his accomplishments were rare because most Holocaust survivors were either physically or psychologically incapable of functioning in the military, let alone earning a Medal of Honor.

No one appreciates America like a war refugee, especially a Jewish one escaping annihilation. As my father, a refugee from persecution himself, used to say repeatedly over the years, "America, I love you." This mindset is part of the Jewish "advantage" you may have over your cohorts. They think they know what patriotism is, but Jews like Rubin (and even my father) understand what it means to be allowed to be yourself without fear.

So, remember this over the High Holy Days which may have a different meaning for you given the past six months. Take a little time each day to separate yourself from your current context and remember who you are and how the Jewish military figures who preceded you helped make your success possible. L'Shanah Tovah tikateivu v'teichateimu—may you be inscribed in the Book of Life for a very good year.

We love you, Norm

Tibor Rubin

Tibor Rubin's liberation from the Mauthausen concentration camp system in Austria during World War II led to a series of events that resulted in his earning the Medal of Honor fifty-five years later. Rubin had been in the Mauthausen camp for over a year when American GIs liberated it in 1945. At that time, he was so grateful that he vowed to repay his debt by becoming a US citizen and a soldier as soon as possible.

Rubin got his wish in 1950 when he found himself fighting in Korea. There, in an act of bravery, he single-handedly defended a hill for twenty-four hours from waves of North Korean soldiers, allowing his regiment to complete a successful withdrawal. A few months later he again distinguished himself in battle when one more time he slowed the enemy's advance and allowed remnants of his unit to retreat safely.

While Rubin had been recommended for America's highest military honor on three occasions, a rabidly anti-Semitic sergeant prevented Rubin from receiving his just due. Unfortunately, it was not uncommon for Jewish soldiers to be subjected to the whims of Jew-hating superiors.

After being taken prisoner by the Chinese in October 1950, Rubin again distinguished himself in the thirty months he was in captivity. While confined, he used the survival skills he'd learned in Mauthausen to save the lives of forty of his fellow prisoners. The communists repeatedly offered liberation to Rubin if he would return to his birthplace of Hungary, but he steadfastly refused. He was an American and he was going to stay that way.

Like many other deserving Jewish veterans who were victims of anti-Semitism in the military, Rubin had to wait—in his case until 2005—to receive his Medal of Honor. However, he never took issue with the perpetrators of this injustice because it was more than enough for him just to be an American. "I always wanted to become a citizen of the United States, and when I became a citizen it was one of the happiest days of my life. I think about the United States and I am a lucky person to live here. When I came to America, it was the first time I was free. It was one of the reasons I joined the US Army, because I wanted to show my appreciation."

•

I couldn't resist sending Greg a picture of the next German Jew's World War I fighter, which has a swastika insignia on the fuselage. Obviously, the symbol had a different meaning back then, but the image triggered some substantial cognitive dissonance in me when looking at it.

The pilot was such a superpatriot that when Germany surrendered after the armistice was signed in 1918, he refused to turn in his beloved airplane. Instead, he flew it to Switzerland to keep it out of the hands of the Allies.

His stubbornness and resistance to authority were familiar qualities, which in part furthered the survival of the Jewish people. While these traits can be self-defeating, in most circumstances throughout Jewish history, they have been beneficial. My father possessed these qualities, many times to a fault, but overall I think they helped him succeed in a tough world. I also know, for a fact, that Greg has them and that they have helped propel him toward his goals.

10/01/2005

Dear Greg,

I seriously debated whether to send you the enclosed Jewish military figure of the week because of the obvious, but the irony was too much to resist. I find it fascinating how easy it was, and is, for people to deny the reality of Jewish military contributions, often to the degree of complete extinction.

Although the Nazis made an art form of this historical distortion, the same dynamic was present in many countries in which Jews served with distinction including our own. I can't help but wonder what Hitler would have said about this picture. Trick photography by his political opponents to embarrass him? At least we know the truth.

Here is another example of Jewish irreverence for authority. I know that it is wrong (in most cases) but the Jew in me is proud of the statement of patriotism that Beckhardt (and later Joe Klein) made by their actions. Fritz and Joe would be pleased with your progress even if you don't abscond with a plane or disregard a direct order from a superior officer.

Carol and I had a great time with you. I really loved the humor that your class showed at track-select. You really fit right in. I especially liked watching you with the other T-38 trainees. It looked like y'all were having a great time and I'm sure that this will continue throughout the remainder of your training.

Love, Norm

Fritz Beckhardt

Fritz Beckhardt was from Wallertheim in Hesse. At the start of the First World War, he volunteered for the infantry and later trained as a pilot in Hamburg and Hanover. He flew long-range reconnaissance missions and later received fighter pilot training and served with Jagdgeschwader 3, Jagdstaffel 26, and Kest 2. During the war Beckhardt received the Iron Cross (First Class), the House Order of Hohenzollern with Swords, the Hessian Medal of Bravery, the Hessian Order of Ernst Ludwig, the aviator's badge, a silver cup for bravery, and various badges for accomplishments and wounds.

•

Growing up, Greg's experiences with anti-Semitism were relatively rare and benign. As a result, I thought that these letters could be used to sensitize him to other Jews in the military who were less fortunate. Greg had asked for advice on how to acknowledge Yom Kippur, the Day of Atonement, which is the holiest day on the Jewish calendar. Jews generally use this day as a time of reflection on the past year and to contemplate how to improve themselves in the coming year. Even the most liberal of practicing Jews fast and take this day off from work or school.

To the credit of the Air Force, a training officer asked Greg if he needed the day off. When Greg declined the offer, the officer remarked that he was glad Greg was not like those "New York Jews" who always asked for the day off. Well, since I was one of those New York Jews who doesn't work on Yom Kippur, the comment flew all over me. However, I never gave Greg's decision a second thought, knowing that he would keep his Jewish identity intact in any event.

The World War II airman referred to in the letter below is one of the members of the Pyramid of Jewish Military Heroes. He was one of Greg's inspirations growing up in Congregation Shaareth Israel in Lubbock, Texas. He was awarded the Distinguished Flying Cross along with his B-29 crew for their extremely dangerous low-level bombing missions over Japan in 1945. I loved and respected his modesty about his wartime experiences as well as his great sense of humor.

In spite of the fact that Jews have received their fair share of Medals of Honor since the Civil War, it took an Act of Congress and, in some cases, fifty or more years to rectify the prevalence of racism and anti-Semitism and honor the heroism of minority servicemen. An example was the Defense Authorization Act, which was sanctioned to review the combat records of Jewish American and Hispanic veterans of World War II, Korea, and Vietnam. The fact that this act was required to set the record straight about Jewish military participation offered Greg some perspective on the challenges his forebears had to confront. Research indicated that a number of Jewish recipients of the Distinguished Service Cross should have been nominated for the Medal of Honor.

As a result, the Leonard Kravitz Jewish War Veterans Act of 2001 was proposed. While it was not adopted, its consideration led Congress to direct the armed forces to reexamine past practices in selecting Medal of Honor recipients.

10/06/2005

Dear Greg,

Enclosed you'll find a brief synopsis of the heroism which earned these three Jews the Medal of Honor in WWII. Their accomplishments were made even greater by the context of the times when Jewish military contributions were so undervalued. In fact, it took an act of Congress to initiate a study into the reasons for there being so many minority (including Tibor Rubin) Korean War vets who earned high medals but never made the ultimate cut to Medal of Honor stature. You can get a good idea from these summaries that Jews were every bit as courageous and honorable as their Gentile counterparts. How dare anyone question our courage, selflessness and dedication to their duty! The fact that Zussman, Jackman and Solomon died while saving others in the war which literally saved Western Civilization makes it that much more meaningful.

You asked about what you could do to affirm your identity on Yom Kippur. I suggested skipping a meal but you might want to add taking a moment to think about these three men (and maybe even say Kaddish for them. It's in the WWII prayer book that I sent). They and many other Jewish heroes may not have anyone to say this prayer of mourning for them and it is customary at Yizkor to memorialize all those dead who have no one to remember them. Even a gesture as small as this can make a big difference in how you feel this day.

I know that you are glad that I didn't overreact to what the training officer said. Bernie Barasch, who has his own relevant stories, said it best: "Keep a low profile during your training and at the end of it you can tell anyone who gave you a hard time to kiss your (Jewish) ass."

So, have a "Gut Yontov" any way you see fit.

Love, Norm

Bernie Barasch

Bernie earned his DFC for being part of a B-29 crew that flew multiple dangerous low-level bombing missions over Japan during World War II. He also shot down a Japanese Zero over Singapore in 1945.

•

There is an old anecdote about a young Jewish draftee who is pressed into the Russian Army. He was religiously observant and kept kosher, so he went to his rabbi to see what advice he could receive about his diet while in an army that relied heavily on pork as a dietary staple. The rabbi calmly advised him not to suck the bones.

While no one knows the exact origin of the kosher laws, they have served the world Jewish community well by ensuring that assimilation into adopted countries and cultures would be minimized. Greg does not keep kosher, but as the years have passed I have noticed that he is paying increased attention to the practice. He no longer eats pork.

You are what you eat, so being mindful of kashrut (the Jewish dietary laws) could only facilitate Greg's strengthening Jewish identity, as it did for so many others—warriors and civilians alike over the thirty-five-hundred-year course of Jewish history.

I thought that this was a good time in this narrative to honor Greg's paternal grandfather.

10/10/2005

Dear Greg,

I wish I had gotten his letter (enclosed) about a Jewish soldier celebrating Yom Kippur in a combat zone to you sooner. I thought it was timely and very touching. It came from a book of war letters, which has been very poignant reading.

I added an enclosure because of our phone call last night when we discussed

Kashrut. The main point of the Kosher laws is to remind us not to act in an ungodly manner which will add to the pain and suffering in the world. It's interesting that the Kosher animals are all herbivorous essentially meaning that people should not harm (eat) each other (metaphorically).

I feel good about your discussing these issues. Doing this can only define your Jewish identities in any way you choose, and strengthen you.

Love, Norm

Sam Levenson

While Greg knew of his grandfather's distinguished military service, Sam had never spoken in detail of it until Greg was in the Air Force. Then Greg cajoled Sam into relating an oral history of his wartime experiences which he recorded with Sam's consent. I was fortunate to have had the opportunity to hear it.

Sam was a navigator on a C-47 transport plane that dropped airborne troops into occupied Europe. On one mission, Sam solemnly told of how thirty-six planes went out, each carrying twenty men, but only eighteen returned. Sam's reluctance to talk about the war and his role in it, as with so many other veterans, is understood.

•

During the time that my uncle Irv Margolis, or "Pudge" as we called him, spent in the Aleutian Islands (mostly underground, by the way), he had the presence of mind to photograph at least one of each class of aircraft he serviced. Fast-forward sixty years to Greg's flight training days. I told Pudge about Greg's goal, and he offered the pictures he took for part of the Air Force scrapbook Greg was keeping. (In true Navy fashion, after his death Pudge had his ashes cast upon the ocean by the Neptune Society.)

Small acts like these, some from unheralded people like Uncle Pudge, became part of the support system from which Greg benefited. He began to see how, through his own accomplishments, he was adding to the historical record.

Milt Margolis, Pudge's brother, was the most military minded of the three Margolis brothers who served simultaneously during World War II. He served with the 6th Armored Division, enjoyed attending their reunions for years after the war, and he loved being involved in veterans' affairs. Milt, among all those in my extended family, would have taken the most pride in Greg.[17]

While compiling information about my uncle's war record, I happened to notice that his Bronze Star was not awarded until 1967. As discussed earlier, the reason for the delay may well have been anti-Semitism among US officers that prejudiced their judgment regarding the combat accomplishments of Jews under their commands. As a result, when it was discovered that a disproportionately low number of Jewish veterans were receiving their well-deserved medals, formal inquiries had to be established to review their records. Apparently, Uncle Milt's record was one of them. He was not awarded his Bronze Star until twenty-two years after World War II.

Being the extraordinarily gracious patriot that he was, he never complained.

---

17 Milt's interest in military affairs ran long and deep. He related to me a story about an elderly uncle of his who was impressed into the Russian Army as a water boy during the Crimean War of 1848. He was eight years old. This practice of taking children from their homes to serve the czar was not uncommon at the time.

10/15/2005

Dear Greg,

As much as I resent the Vietnam War to this day, I was glad to see that we were represented in the air, and so ably I might add. Actually, I read something recently which said that there were "thousands of Jews who served in Vietnam." The point here is not the validity of the war but that the U.S. was at war and that Jews were represented and accounted very well for themselves.

Regarding the medals I felt that it was time for you to be the official custodian of some of my family's military history. Irv Margolis, or Pudge as we affectionately called him, is probably the most modest, unassuming and passive person I've ever known. Like so many other WWII vets he didn't even bother to pick up his medals after the war. As you remember I wrote for them. He earned them so they sent them. They are authentic reproductions of the actual medals given in 1945-6.

The connection to flight is that Pudge's main job in the Navy was the fueling and servicing of Naval aircraft in the Aleutian Islands. He was stationed on both Attu and Kiska for about 18 months. Take a look on a globe about where these islands are. You could not find a more godforsaken area on earth where the war was conducted. Anyway, he will be proud to know that you have these and are representing your country in the way you are doing.

Fortunately, the Shulman-Margolis family military history is not solely represented by my uncle Leon's (two) busts in rank. As you may remember Uncle Milt (a 3rd brother) received a bronze star as a combat medic in Europe, which along with his military experience was the defining moment in his life.

Certainly most in my family would not qualify as military heroes but no one can say that they weren't there or did not do their part.

With much pride and love, Norm

Milt Margolis

Sgt. Margolis, recipient of the Bronze Star for courage under fire as a combat medic in the European theatre during World War II, came to his role very reluctantly. He told the story of how medics were in short supply and many more were needed after D-Day. One day he and his buddies from the 6th Armored Division were lined up and asked to count off. Every fourth one would be selected out and sent for medic training. Milt was very determined at that time to carry a rifle and get in the fighting, so he tried to predict the count and put himself in line to remain an infantry soldier. He got caught and was ordered to medic training with a vengeance.

Milt hated the Nazis for what they did to his beloved soldiers of the 6th, whom he struggled to save. His contempt for the Nazis was so great that fifty years later, when American helmets were redesigned to

Irv Margolis, the author's uncle, with his mother in 1943. Irv Margolis photographed many naval aircraft he serviced while stationed on Attu during World War II. Prior to his death, he gave all the pictures to Greg as a UPT graduation present.

Milton Margolis, highly decorated uncle of the author, who distinguished himself in combat in World War II.

include ear coverings that resembled those of German Army helmets, he had an absolute fit. Better that the ears of American soldiers be less protected than for them to wear helmets that resembled those of his former adversary.

An Incorrigible Child

"The response to an incorrigible child is to love the child more than ever."

—Jewish proverb

GREG WAS A GOOD STUDENT WHO ATTENDED A VERY competitive "Blue Ribbon" high school in Lubbock, Texas. So at times he needed help. My strength was English, and it came in very handy. I relished the time we spent together going over various challenging English assignments. Tuesday was vocabulary night.

Greg was never academically lax. Since his career goals were well within his reach, I never had to push him. I tried to set an example through my passion for my work and the self-discipline required to be successful.

At the same time, I was actively working on reinforcing a positive and strong Jewish identity. I helped prepare him for his Bar Mitzvah and encouraged him to complete confirmation classes, some of which I taught. Carol and I knew that someday his spiritual foundation would be tested, as it certainly was.

I think I have been unfair to my parents by emphasizing the impact their benign neglect had on me. Their parenting should not be defined by this dynamic. They mostly got it right.

Thinking back, my mother not only maintained a household of as many as seven family members, she also worked full-time at the restaurant. After making us breakfast and then cooking all day at the Driftwood Lounge, she would come home and prepare a delicious dinner for all of us. She did this while ensuring that all our laundry would be done and that the house was clean. Mom never complained, and I clearly took her for granted.

Growing up, my responsibilities were limited to lawn mowing, garbage detail, and snow removal. I was never expected to work in the restaurant; other plans had been laid out for me. I can't say I was spoiled, but I can see why others might think so.

My parents were conditioned from an early age to do all within their power to set us up for a better life. They were as generous as parents could be without giving us a sense of entitlement. The three of us kids were eventually more appreciative, and I know we were successful in passing this value on to the next generation.

I used to tell Greg that I made a good stepfather by doing the opposite of what my father did. I was really only referring to education. Too much of my future decision-making was left up to me by my parents not taking the reins themselves. However, their openheartedness and giving spirit weighed much more significantly on my development than their hands-off parenting style.

Two vivid memories of their generosity stand out. When I was in junior high school and went to buy my first serious baseball glove, I knew exactly what I wanted, picked it out at the sporting goods store, and presented it at the counter. It cost twenty-eight dollars, a considerable sum in those days.

My father opened his wallet and found only twenty-five dollars. Sorry, not enough, so we returned to our car. There I sat not complaining but looking so disappointed that my father noticed. He thought for a second, got out of the car, and returned to the store where the owner was closing.

Pop pushed his way into the store, left the twenty-five dollars on the counter, took the glove, and left with it. The proprietor, apparently sensing the situation, gave my father a pass. Pop made me the happiest of kids that day, but it is for much more than the glove that I am grateful. This small—and in retrospect quite funny—act of love and blind devotion struck me later in life as symbolic of what Pop had difficulty expressing openly. As a result, I realized how important it would be to emulate him when I became a parent.

I have calculated that my education cost about $60,000, or about $250,000 in today's dollars. Pop never complained about the cost until I decided in graduate school that he had done enough. Enough to him was support to the completion of my degree, whatever that degree might be. He was upset when I took out loans for the last years of school because he didn't want me to have any debt, but it just didn't seem right for him to keep funding me.

Pop found it easier to give materially than emotionally. As I began to need less of him moneywise, he became frustrated. Once on my way back to Boston after a visit I recall his standing on a second-floor balcony of his apartment to say good-bye. He again asked if I needed anything (money), to which I said no. He asked me to wait a second and went into the apartment. He returned, leaned over the railing, and said, "Take this." He dropped an apple.

As stated earlier in this book, the Jewish War Veterans of the United States of America was founded in response to the general consensus at the time (1896) that Jews did not fight during the Civil War. A historical survey of vets on both sides proved this popular misconception wrong. Mark Twain, perhaps trying to atone for his previous anti-Semitic comments, chimed in and wrote in the *Harper's Magazine* of March 1898 of the Jewish overrepresentation as participants in the Civil War; more Jews served per capita than in the general population. I thought the selection for the next letter of a Union veteran with a Medal of Honor was ample evidence of a stereotype proved grossly inaccurate.

10/17/2005

Dear Greg,

I know you have precious little time for yourself so I'll keep the next series of letters and its heroes short. I know you've gotten the point but it will be fun to run the course and get to graduation with at least one hero per week accounted for.

One of the reasons for the Zionist movement which led to the formation of the state of Israel was that it occurred to many that too many Jews were put in the position of killing other Jews in times of war, such as WWI. The reasoning went that if they were going to die in battle it may as well be for their own country.

The Civil War was another conflict in which Jews found themselves pitted against each other. The Talmud instructs us to fight for one's country but the thought of Jew vs. Jew bothers many Jews nonetheless, partly due to our relatively low numbers.

For some reason I find the war letters
from the Civil War the saddest of all probably because it was literally brother vs.
brother in many cases. I wonder if Abe
Cohn thought about the irony of possibly
killing Confederate Jews. Anyway, Abe was
awarded his Medal of Honor after all the
Medal of Honor cases were reviewed. His
held up so here he is.

Love, Norm

Abraham Cohn

Abraham Cohn was one of four Jews to win the MOH for "conspicuous gallantry and rallying and forming, under heavy fire, disorga-
nized and fleeing troops of different regiments" at the Battle of the
Wilderness in 1864 and Petersburg.

Cohn convinced and motivated soldiers from retreating broken
units, who did not recognize his authority, to stand and fight advancing Confederate forces. The defensive line he organized brought the
Confederate counteroffensive to a halt.

•

Here is an interesting story about this week's hero, better known as
"Murderous Manny." He died in 1998 and was honored in the *New
York Times* with a long obit citing his impressive World War II exploits.
He is best known for saving the life (in aerial combat) of Capt. James
Swett, a great Marine pilot who earned the Medal of Honor for shoot-
ing down seven Japanese fighters in one sortie.

The story goes that these two fearless Marines were flying together
when they accidentally came in contact with approximately forty

Japanese warplanes. Twenty-to-one odds, just about even money for a couple of Leathernecks. Both survived to tell the tale, which is well worth looking up. The Jewish pilot finished the war with twelve air victories to his credit.

```
                                        10/24/2005

  Dear Greg,


  It took a lot of digging, but I was finally
  able to get at least one name I have been
  searching for. Behold a great WWII Jewish
  ace. Again it is personally gratifying to
  learn of such men at a time when Jews
  were being murdered and unable to help
  themselves. Segal's success is even more
  significant when you study history and
  learn that few countries and individuals
  were willing to try to do something about
  the Holocaust. This guy did. Usually, the
  U.S. does the right thing to help people in
  need and it is comforting to know that you
  will be part of those efforts in some way.
     Have a blast in the T-38 and think of
  your predecessors when you do.

                                    Love, Norm
```

Harold Segal[18]

Harold Segal, a Marine fighter pilot who shot down 12 Japanese planes in World War II, three of them in a single duel that ended

18 Richard Goldstein, "Harold Segal, World War II Hero, Dies at 77," *New York Times*, June 9, 1998.

with his being fished out of the Pacific Ocean by an American destroyer, died on Wednesday at his home in Scottsdale, Ariz. He was 77.

In March 1944, more than 500 people, including Army, Navy and Marine officers and the Manhattan Borough President, Edgar Harvey Jr., gathered at the Hotel Pennsylvania in Manhattan to honor Lieutenant Segal, a former art student from New York, on his triumphant return home. The Marine ace and winner of the Distinguished Flying Cross had an extraordinary tale for them.

The odds had been overwhelming back on July 11, 1943, when Lieutenant Segal and seven other pilots from Marine Fighting Squadron 221 had taken off in single-engine Corsair fighters that the Japanese called Whistling Death to escort American bombers over Rendova Island in the Solomons. Then six pilots returned to base with faulty engines, leaving only Lieutenant Segal and Capt. James Swett to continue the mission.

When they spotted at least 40 Japanese Zero fighters and bombers at 25,000 feet, Captain Swett, who would win the Medal of Honor for having downed seven Japanese planes in a single encounter the previous April, dived toward the bombers. Lieutenant Segal followed in a fighter he had named Ruthie in honor of his mother. The Zeros then got on the Americans' tails, but just as one opened fire on Captain Swett, Lieutenant Segal shot it down.

Before pulling out of his dive, Lieutenant Segal spotted two Zeros to his left.

"I caught the top Zero first," he reported soon afterward. "He blew up like matchwood. The second Zero never knew what hit him. My dive practically carried me into his cockpit with all guns blazing. He hit the sea a mass of flaming wreckage."

While passing through a layer of Japanese bombers on his dive, Lieutenant Segal's plane was hit by a long burst of fire. Four Zeroes then pursued him, and two peppered his plane, sending it plunging into the Pacific 10 miles off New Georgia Island at 110 miles an hour.

His plane sank in 20 seconds, but his injuries were minor: a broken nose, two cracked front teeth and a cut on his upper lip. He freed himself, inflated his life jacket and spent 22 hours in the ocean, killing a sea gull for his only source of food, before being picked up by a destroyer.

"He was waving and yelling but the ship passed him by," Mr. Segal's son, Robb, recalled. "A man on the end of the boat then looked back and happened to see him. The ship had orders not to turn around for anyone, but it did."

The destroyer hauled Lieutenant Segal in with a rope and let him off on Guadalcanal. He tried to learn the identity of the sailor who had spotted him, hoping to offer thanks for saving his life, but he never found out the man's name.

Upon his return home in 1944 as a captain, he was introduced to reporters at the Marines' public relations office in New York.

Asked how he was able to survive after having been shot down, he replied, "A man named God was sitting beside me."

His fellow pilots nicknamed him Murderous Mannie after his exploits on July 11, 1943. As his son explained it, "His father's name was Mannie, and Murderous Mannie sounded a lot tougher than Murderous Harold." The sobriquet stuck over the years, but Mr. Segal came to be amused at the fuss that had been made over his heroics.

A friend, Col. R. Bruce Porter, himself a Marine air ace in World War II, remembered what Mr. Segal had said a few years ago when asked how he managed to down three Zeros that day in July 1943.

"I really didn't shoot them down," he said. "They just got in my way when I was going home."

•

I felt compelled to inform Greg of what I knew about Air Force evangelism even though by this time he was confident that he could handle any situation in which he was being proselytized. I added the name of this naval officer who ensured that in spite of any military environment a Jew might find himself in, there would always be someone who would be there to affirm Jewish identity. Although not a combat hero, he was a hero in his own right.

11/01/2005

Dear Greg,

I thought the enclosed was interesting. The armed services seem to vary in their relationships with minority religions and unfortunately the Air Force has the worst record. Carol and I watched a Tom Brokaw TV special about the growing evangelist movement. There is a mega church (6,000 members) close to the Air Force Academy where many of the cadets attend. There is almost a cult-like quality to churches like these, which gives me the creeps. The born-again cadets share this creepiness. They possess this almost faraway look in their eyes and there is a brainwashed quality to the way they proselytize to "non-converted" Christians.

Some Christians frequently cross the fine line between their obligations to spread the word and showing tolerance for others and their influence in right-wing politics is undeniable. I know that you can handle these guys, but I hope you never have to. I'm assuming that most of this kind of thing will be well behind you by the time you join the 150th.

I'm not sure if Commander Baumwald is a hero in the true sense of the word but he certainly stands in high esteem for taking the responsibility of leading lay services on the [USS *Carl*] *Vinson*. It gives me comfort in my advancing age that thousands of Jewish servicemen have the opportunity of freely expressing their faith wherever they happen to be! There is no better reason to fight for your country.

Love, Norm

P.S. Have I ever told you the story of how I led Yom Kippur services on a cruise ship?

Steven Baumwald

During the past two years Americans have come to depend greatly on the skill and patriotism of our armed forces. While it is difficult to imagine the courage it takes to put your life on the line and leave your home and family behind, it is also difficult to comprehend being in harm's way and away from home during holidays of all kinds—including, for Jewish servicepersons, Shabbat and the High Holy days.

Here is an opportunity for you to help. The US Navy is in need of Jewish religious items—they can be new or gently used and what is needed runs the gamut from Kiddush cups to Shabbat candlesticks, Challah covers to Likrat Shabbat Siddurim, and Machzorim. If you, your family, your school, or your synagogue would like to help with this project, please mail your items to:

Office of the Chaplain
MCAS Miramar
San Diego, CA 92145

Steve Baumwald (L) and Robert
Krigelman, Jewish lay leader aboard
the USS *Carl Vinson* aircraft carrier,
home-ported in San Diego, Califor-
nia. (Photo permission courtesy of
Cmdr. Steven Baumwald (Ret.).)

On ships in the Gulf and across the seas there are Jewish service-men in need of a little taste of home during the holidays and on Shabbat. Your donation of an item will go a long way in letting them know they are not forgotten at this joyous time of year.

(The above was submitted by Steve Baumwald, who was a pilot and commander in the US Naval Reserve. He served active duty as a naval pilot in the first Gulf War and led services weekly for himself and the other Jewish servicemen aboard the USS *Carl Vinson*.)

Before God on Judgment Day

"When one stands before God on Judgment Day, one is accountable not just for what sins have been committed but also for failing to use the gifts God has bestowed."

—Jewish proverb

AS LONG AS I'VE WORKED WITH PEOPLE, WHICH as of this writing has been for about fifty years, give or take, I have always been fascinated by how small events can alter one's life course. My early struggle with math and chemistry completely redirected the life I and others had set for me.

I should have known earlier that my poor math skills would have forecasted my inability to go to medical school. As it was, I went into tenth grade ignorant of the impact a bad grade in a key subject could have on my future aspirations.

Geometry was my nemesis. I had no chance to pass it. I failed to catch on in the beginning. Week by week went by, and I fell further and further behind. It got so bad that my teacher, who was actually quite nice, moved me to a separate table and chair apart from the regular class. However, she made no effort to secure extra help for me.

My parents finally got a tutor for me, but it was much too late. I got a 31 in the course, and for all intents and purposes my thoughts of medical school dissipated. I still don't know how I passed the course in summer school.

Anyway, dreams are fleeting and without realizing it at the time, mine was gone. Flunking chemistry as a college freshman only sealed the deal. Who knows whether more attention to my struggle—from the school or my parents—would have made a difference? In retrospect I consider these failures as positive because I was forced to pursue another profession, one I was much more suited to do.

In November 1978 in Boston, life finally started getting better. I got my first full-time professional position. I was hired by a community mental health center in Concord, New Hampshire, to do crisis intervention out of a general hospital emergency center. Here I found meaning and purpose. I was temperamentally suited for crisis work because I thrived on the opportunity to quickly make a difference in people's lives at their lowest points.

As I learned this aspect of mental health interventions, it did not escape me that I was fulfilling the Jewish mandate of *tikkun olam*, or healing the world. Occasionally, I would reflect on this obligation when I was asked to get up at 3 a.m. in minus-twenty-degree weather. I remember vividly what my car seat felt like when I sat in it before the drive to the hospital. My faith never failed to get me through these situations when I needed to call upon it.

However, along with performing the standard crisis intervention duties, I was introduced to an aspect of emergency services I was totally unprepared for: assisting the police during first-responder situations. I never gave a thought to the possibility of psychology as a potentially life-threatening profession, and it did not help that in some ways the police weren't fully prepared either.

I suppose it may have been a compliment for my supervisor to assume that I would make my way functioning in critical incidents. On the other hand, these experiences became an extension of what I grew up with, expectations without preparation. The police had yet to figure out their SWAT protocol, so our crisis team and the cops learned by doing. On no fewer than four interventions I was asked to step in with unstable individuals with "hot" weapons. When I went in I don't remember being afraid; I was anxious and full of adrenaline, but not fearful. I never hesitated to answer a call and assist the police in these dangerous situations.

I remember two telling examples of how unprepared we as first responders were in those days. During one intervention I went to a site where an intoxicated man had threatened someone with a shotgun. After the police and I arrived, I was asked to position myself in a relatively exposed area to talk to the individual through a megaphone in order to distract him while the police entered the building.

As we were setting up for the confrontation I turned to an officer who was putting on a bulletproof vest and other protective gear. I asked him where I could get similar equipment to protect myself, assuming that the gear was general issue. To my surprise and dismay, he informed me that he was given his by his girlfriend as a Christmas gift. No general-issue gear was available. I took my megaphone, hid myself as best I could, and did what I do best: talk.

The second example was equally unnerving. I don't know anyone but me who deliberately has gone out of his way to get stopped for speeding by the police. I was called into a situation that involved another intoxicated individual with a loaded rifle threatening suicide. As I indicated earlier our training was limited, and I was very nervous about going in alone. As a result, I thought it only made sense for me to go in with a police escort, but none had been assigned to accompany me. So I thought I'd get my own escort.

I began speeding through the streets of Concord, New Hampshire, on my way to the site and finally attracted the attention of a police officer who thankfully pulled me over. I frantically told him my story, which he quickly verified, and he waved me on. I breathed a sigh of relief and looked into the rearview mirror now confident that I would have adequate protection—only to my surprise the cop did an abrupt 180 and sped away. I went in alone anyway, but a lot more slowly.

I thought, whenever feasible, I would use examples such as these to show Greg that to some degree I was courageous. What parent doesn't want their children to think of them as having fortitude under difficult circumstances? This was especially important given the reality of his goal to enter into combat. Not that there is much of a comparison, but it is at least suggestive of "courage under fire."

Since my job has more to do with emotional strength and resilience, I wanted to set an example with these qualities as well. These traits would serve Greg in life and need to be accessed much more than physical courage.

Greg was in combat in Iraq in 2007, and on four occasions he bombed structures and vehicles. He said he never knew if he killed anyone, which seemed to be somewhat of a relief to him. I, on the other hand, never having been in combat, am fully aware that I took a life.

I was on call one night in the hospital when I was notified that an eighteen-year-old Jewish male was being brought in with a severe head injury sustained in a motor vehicle accident. He was a college student from Baltimore on his way to Winter Carnival at Dartmouth in Hanover, New Hampshire, about an hour or so north of Concord.

The boy had essentially flatlined, but his parents wanted to hang on as long as there was the slightest chance of recovery. Eleven days later, confronted with a flat EEG and devoid of hope, the parents chose disconnection, praying that their son would quickly expire.

Each of the parents approached the dreaded moment very differently. The father wanted no part of the actual cord pulling. The mother, on the other hand, wanted to be part of her son's death. However, she didn't want to do it alone. I volunteered.

So together, her hand over mine, we pulled. Mercifully, the young man died instantly. This was one of the most difficult things—if not the most difficult—I have ever done. What helped to sustain and guide me during this ordeal was my faith, which clearly mandates that the alleviation of suffering is a primary responsibility whenever possible.

When Greg was accepted for flight training, I teased him about now being a member of the second-best air force in the world. Whether this is true or not, Jews worldwide take great pride in the Israeli Air Force and its remarkable history protecting the State of Israel. Air superiority is an enormous advantage that Israel's enemies should never again challenge. Nor should it be taken for granted.

Pilots like the next one will help ensure that neither happens. I still hope that Greg has the pleasure of meeting Israeli pilots and the opportunity to share all that they have in common, militarily and spiritually.

11/08/2005

Dear Greg,

Below briefly describes one of the greatest feats of aviation history. It becomes especially important and it is unlikely to ever be repeated. Iran's newest Islamo-Fascist leader, the one calling for the destruction of Israel, called the Israelis out and challenged them to repeat what they did in Iraq and more recently in Syria. It must be tempting for the Israelis, but the element of surprise is long gone and the Iranian nuclear facilities are deeply buried. As I've suggested before I think that it would be cool for you to meet some Israeli pilots at Operation Red Flag. They are reportedly a bit crusty and difficult to get to know

at first, but once the ice is broken they
are regular guys. They need to see that
Diaspora Jews are doing their part in the
air and that the tie between you and them
is undeniable and eternal.

Love, Norm

Iftach Spector

Brig. Gen. Iftach Spector was already a triple ace, meaning that he had shot down fifteen enemy aircraft, before he took part in the most important mission of his life. At that time Saddam Hussein was developing a nuclear weapons program that he most certainly would have used to threaten the existence of the State of Israel. In 1981 Gen. Spector flew the raid on the Iraqi Osirak nuclear reactor site. Eight F-16As, with six F-15As acting as a cover, launched a long-range attack by flying at very low altitudes to avoid radar contact. The F-16s, armed with sixteen conventional bombs, all hit their target and destroyed the reactor core before it could be activated. The Iraqi nuclear weapons program never recovered, much to the relief of Israel and the free world.

As stated earlier, Greg is a great admirer of General Hap Arnold, so I thought that he might enjoy learning about Israel's equivalent in every sense of the word. Fifty-six years later, the Israeli Air Force remains unchallenged largely due to the initial inspiration given to it by its founders.

11/14/2005

Dear Greg,

I think it would be fair to say that the
hero below is the "Hap Arnold" of the
Israel Air Force. When Israel was created
they threw together a makeshift Air Force

which accounted well for itself during the
War of Independence in '48-'49. Tolkovski
had vision and shaped the IAF in such a
way that ensured its success to the present
day. And it's good that he did, because as
the IAF goes, so goes Israel—and this is no
exaggeration.

By the time you get this you will have
passed your check ride with flying colors.
Don't ask me how I know these things but I
always have and hopefully always will.

Love, Norm

Dan Tolkowsky

Dan Tolkowsky entered the military in 1943 when the RAF sent a
Jewish unit from Palestine to train at a flight school in Rhodesia. He
was the first in his class to complete the course and become a fighter
and reconnaissance pilot in Greece. After World War II he joined the
nascent Israeli Air Force and assisted in procurement of modern military aircraft from Czechoslovakia.

In 1953 Gen. Tolkowsky was appointed head of the Israeli Air
Force. He quickly recognized that Israel could never match its neighbors in the quantity of aircraft in service and must therefore aim at
superior quality. Accordingly, he put great energy into turning the
IAF into a professional, well-organized, and highly trained service
that has proven itself repeatedly in Israel's War of Independence and
many subsequent wars to maintain its independence. Gen. Newman
recalled that he and Gen. Tolkowsky once shared scotch and war
stories at Stan's home in Oklahoma.

•

As you already are aware, my father was no martial hero, and his military record was the source of family amusement over the years. He did, however, appreciate and love America and would have supported Greg's decision even though it would have been difficult for him to comprehend. Their not ever having met is a source of regret I have to this day.

My niece Janet who has a blown-up picture of my father in his doughboy uniform from World War I. His immigration story reflected that of countless other Eastern European Jews who escaped oppression and the sometimes-unbearable military service that was part of it. No Military Hero of the Week accompanied this letter due to its content.

11/29/2005

Dear Greg,

I enjoy reading about immigrants, like my father's immigrating to the US, and fighting for their new country. As I've told you before, the persecuted and oppressed appreciate freedom much more than most native-born Americans. Janet has a 2-foot x 3-foot picture of my 20-year-old father in the same uniform as the enclosed. I suppose, as fate would have had it my father could have been sent over and maybe I wouldn't be here now.

As for owing me something for the past 15 years I hope that you know I was teasing. You "pay me back" every time I see you and more than you might think. You already repaid your "debt" by becoming the upright, moral and ethical person that you are. Your service and wings only make you that much better. You have the right stuff in more than one way.

Love, Norm

CHAPTER 8

Everything but Good Sense

"Money will buy you everything but good sense."

—Jewish proverb

AS GREG GREW UP, OUR TIMES TOGETHER BECAME less didactic and more fun. I especially enjoyed our alone times around holidays when I would fly to Austin and drive home with him, and as he got closer to serving, discussing military affairs and history.

What I found to be especially rewarding were his spontaneous and totally unexpected invitations for me to go to air shows with him or just have dinner together. I didn't have to try too hard to be a proper parent. With him, less was definitely more.

One of Greg's qualities that made him fun to be with was his self-effacing humor. He was always confident enough to laugh at himself.

For one of Greg's birthdays, I bought him a ride in a glider. I was in the drag plane that carried his glider aloft and then released it at a great height. The glider then gradually descended to the ground in wide lazy circles.

I landed first and watched him come in. He slowly emerged from the glider and walked over to me while carrying a brown paper sack full of what I quickly realized was Greg's vomit. In retrospect it is an even more amusing memory given his success as an F-16 pilot; this experience did not deter him from his dream quest in the slightest.

While West Texas provides wide-open spaces for glider rides, it is also a place where it is a challenge to hold onto a minority identity. These challenges often resurrected memories of events that, in retrospect, helped shape me. They seem to come back to me whenever something happens that reminds me of who I am. One is from the distant past; the other occurred in the early '80s.

I used to go with my father to run errands when I was a kid. One time we went to a junkyard to work out some transaction with the proprietor. He introduced himself as "Mike Sullivan." On the way out of the yard, I turned to him and asked who the hell Mike Sullivan was. He said he used that name in business when he didn't want people to know that he was Jewish. I teased him by indicating that to many, his looks, his nose in particular, would belie the name. He said that apparently it worked well for him because he had been getting away with it for years.

My last visit to see my parents in Syracuse in 1981 was particularly memorable. My father and I went to Sabbath services, and a Bar Mitzvah was in progress. At one point during the ceremony the rabbi was waxing eloquent about the generational continuity of Judaism and how Bar and Bat Mitzvahs (for non-Jewish readers, Bat Mitzvahs are for girls) were fundamental to this phenomenon. The rabbi related his message of the importance of rituals and traditions to Jews who came to America and brought with them a spiritual foundation upon which their descendants could live their lives in strange lands.

In the middle of his discourse the rabbi saw my father among the congregation and pointed him out. The rabbi referred to my father as "authentic," meaning that he carried the essence of his faith with him from Eastern Europe. He stood as an example to future generations about the importance of remaining true to one's traditions and thereby sustaining oneself. All heads in the congregation turned toward him and got the message. While my father was not exceptional in any sense of the word, he was a living example of Jewish resilience and how his faith bolstered him and his people during the Diaspora.

On New Year's Eve 1981, my mother had a major stroke while she and my father were visiting family. They were stuck in Miami. My mother died three years later of complications from her stroke. Pop was forced to sell his beloved bar and never returned to Syracuse until his death and burial in 1993.

Shortly after my mother's death in 1985, the year before I met Greg and Carol, I went on my first cruise. The last day of the cruise fell on Yom Kippur, and I was unsure how to acknowledge it.

On that last day there was an announcement over the ship's loudspeaker: All those wishing to attend Yom Kippur services were invited to a designated room. I went and found about six or seven others who wished to worship. One was a tall, dark-skinned gentleman whom I approached out of curiosity. As it turned out he was an Egyptian Jew. I had never met a Jew from Egypt before.

Jews had largely been forced to emigrate from Egypt in 1948 after the State of Israel was established. Out of a population of approximately seventy-five thousand Jews, only a few hundred remained. How and why was he allowed to stay? Did his family originate from another country from which Jews were expelled, or was he a descendant of an original population of Jews dating back to biblical times? In spite of the fact that I had neglected to ask him these questions in the moment, I was becoming more attuned to future situations that could tell me more about myself and my people. I promised myself not to miss any more historical revelations.

Since the man whose name I forgot and I were the only ones in the room who knew Hebrew, we led the Yom Kippur service. Two Jews from vastly different countries, backgrounds, and experiences came together briefly on common ground.

It is difficult to describe, but over the years I have become more sensitive to anti-Semitic vibrations emanating from people from countries with long histories of Jew hatred. It is subtle but definitely there. So recently, when I saw that a physician from Poland had scheduled an appointment with me, I was a bit apprehensive. The doctor happened to be from my father's hometown, Bialystok, one of the few times I have met someone from that city. I couldn't help but think about the unfortunate anti-Semitic incidents my father and I had there.

As it turned out the physician did not have a shred of anti-Semitism in her. In fact, when she described the tour she had at Auschwitz years before, she wept. From then on, I would try harder to avoid stereotyping; nothing good ever comes from it.

•

It has always irked me when a Jew shows prejudice against another minority. Of all of God's people, we ought to know better. This only goes to show that human frailty transcends ethnic and religious bounds.

I was as proud of this week's hero's postwar courage as I was of his heroism on board the *Canberra* on that fateful day. Courage can manifest in many ways, and while I knew Greg understands this concept, as a parent I thought it never hurt to reinforce it.

12/05/2005

Dear Greg,

I saw my uncle (Irv Margolis) last week and he gave me this last picture to complete "the collection." I'd like to tell you that

this is one of the Doolittle Raiders that
my uncle fueled before that fateful attack
on Tokyo but that would be the stuff of
fiction. It's still a pretty neat group of
pictures and he did work on every one of
these planes.

Love, Norm

Stanley Greenburg

During World War II Stanley Greenburg was on the USS *Canberra* when it took an aerial torpedo near the engine room somewhere in the South Pacific. The blast tore a seventy-five-foot hole in the side of the ship, but somehow it remained afloat. Seaman Greenburg was the last sailor to evacuate the engine room before it flooded.

However, this is not the only reason for which I consider him heroic. The other is that he had the guts to bring home a Japanese bride he met during the post–World War II occupation. He had the courage to face the extreme anti-Japanese prejudice that was so prevalent at the time. The fact that he is a Jew only makes me even more proud to know about him. By the way, as of this writing he is married to the same woman sixty-plus years later.

•

While Greg has earned several academic and athletic awards over the years, the one his mother and I most treasure was the one for "Kindness" that he received in first grade. While his other awards have been packed away, this simple ribbon to this day hangs on our refrigerator. We have always tried to emphasize the relative importance of substantive values over more superficial or material ones, and we are proud to say that Greg has rarely disappointed us.

The next letter speaks to the quality of his character as seen by his reaction to the hypercompetitive atmosphere of flight school. Greg has never shied away from empathizing with the underdog, whether a classmate struggling with the hazing of Undergraduate Pilot Training or the innocent casualties of war he was later exposed to in Iraq.

I doubt that he or most other Jews have appreciated the efforts of the partisans who fought as behind-the-lines civilian combatants as reflected by the three heroes of this week. From a military perspective there was not a fighting group with more disadvantages to overcome, yet they did more than their share during World War II. As with most veterans they didn't talk much about their wartime experiences, so their accomplishments were relatively unappreciated.

The next time you are with an elderly relative who was in occupied Europe at the time of World War II and who may not have been in uniform, dare ask the question about their part in the war. You might be very surprised by what you discover.

12/12/2005

Dear Greg,

The intent of these letters is to give you something to fall back on in times of need and I am pleased that you are using them for this reason. By the time we complete this historical exercise at UPT gradua-tion, your legacy should be strong enough to keep you going in the most difficult of circumstances such as in survival school.

I have always emphasized that I am proud of you for your character more than your flying. This was again borne out when you told me how much the competitive atmo-sphere at UPT bothered you. You can be as competitive as you need to be without turning into an asshole. It will be a relief for you to be able to get back to being your sweet old low-key self in a few months.

Regarding this week's heroes, it has always bothered me that partisans or guerilla fighters never get the credit they deserve, for their training was next to nothing, they were poorly equipped and clothed, and they had the disadvantage of having to worry about getting killed by other anti-Semitic partisan groups.

Remember they did not have to fight. They could have remained hidden for the duration of the war and no one would have thought less of them. They fought because they could and after hearing about and seeing the abuse their people had to endure over the centuries they fought extremely well. They were not sheep for the slaughter as all Jews were depicted by some. Rather they were wolves who fought well beyond their means.

Love, Norm

Abba Kovner, Vitka Kempner, and Ruzka Korczak

This week's heroes were in their teens and gave the Nazis fits because of the behind-the-lines havoc they caused. I am proud to say that the first Nazi train blown up after the occupation of Eastern Europe was executed by a seventeen-year-old Jewish woman, Vitka Kempner, in one of these partisan units. These three heroes may never be recognized as such, but they were true heroes nonetheless. All survived the war and settled in Israel, where they used their military skills to help found a nation. Kovner served as a commander during the War of Independence in 1948–1949. He survived that war, too. All were effective resistance fighters. May the contributions of these three be forever etched in history.

> Hitler is plotting to destroy all European Jews. Lithuanian Jews will be the first in line. Let us not be led like sheep to the slaughterhouse. It is right, we are weak and without defense, but the only answer to the enemy is resistance!
>
> —Abba Kovner

·

In spite of Greg's busy schedule I thought that a more detailed account of a Jewish warrior's exploits would be additional inspiration. Lawrence Freedman was a warrior.

Only very rarely would a Jew hide his identity. Even if the name was changed to hopefully forestall any potential problems, a Jew would say who he was and deal with the consequences rather than deny it altogether. In the course of this research I never found a Jew who denied his identity.

12/25/2005

```
Dear Greg,

As far as breaking a negative Jewish stereo-
type of passivity this guy takes the cake.
Men like him are generally Jewish in name
only but they rarely, if ever, deny their
Jewishness. They often try to turn it into
```

a positive as Freedman did. I'm not sure I would want to befriend a guy like this, but I sure am proud of his accomplishments and courage.

Only four months to go and I'm still not running out of names. You're now over the hump and on the downhill side of your training. Each day brings you closer to your goal and we continue to enjoy every detail about the process.

Much love, Happy Chanukah and fly well into the New Year.

Love, Norm

Lawrence N. Freedman[19]

GREENSBURG, Pennsylvania—Friends of the only American to be killed so far during the U.S. military relief mission to Somalia say the Fayetteville, North Carolina, man may have had covert responsibilities along with his civilian duties.

Friends of former Green Beret Lawrence N. Freedman said Freedman had kept in touch with the Special Forces in the years since he left active duty to become a civilian employee of the Army, the Greensburg *Tribune-Review* reported Tuesday.

Freedman, 51, was buried Tuesday at Arlington National Cemetery in Virginia following a funeral service at the Army chapel at nearby Fort Meyer.

---

19 US Army press report, December 30, 1992, http://www.arlingtoncemetery.net/lnfreedman.htm. See also Lt. Gen. Daniel Bolger, US Army (ret.), "The Outpost: The Life and Death of a 'Quiet Professional,'" Association of the US Army, December 15, 2017, https://www.ausa.org/articles/outpost-life-and-death-%E2%80%98quiet-professional%E2%80%99.

He was killed last Wednesday near Bardera when the vehicle he was riding struck an anti-tank mine. Three State Department officials were injured.

"He was a soldier's soldier," said longtime friend Arthur Lacey. "He had a lot of influence over a lot of men—all positive."

Some of those interviewed by the newspaper spoke only on the condition that they not be identified by name.

"He was always someplace where nobody knew where he was," a childhood friend told the newspaper. "He was always in the forefront of what was happening."

Freedman grew up in Philadelphia and at the time of his death lived near Fort Bragg, North Carolina, headquarters of Army special forces.

He enlisted in the Army on September 30, 1965, and served for 25 years, said Joyce Wiesner, a spokesman at the Army Reserve Personnel Center in St. Louis. A medical specialist, Freedman retired December 31, 1990, with the rank of sergeant major.

Freedman served in Vietnam for two years and earned two Bronze Stars and a Purple Heart, Wiesner said.

After participating in six campaigns in Vietnam, Freedman was stationed for several years in Okinawa, Wiesner said.

Acquaintances said Freedman was involved in intelligence work in connection with the U.S. dispute with Libya and also during the Falklands war, in which the United States backed Great Britain's effort against Argentina.

They said Freedman was secretive about his military duties. They said they thought he was a member of the Delta Force, a rapid-deployment unit, and that he probably had covert responsibilities in Somalia.

State Department officials referred questions about Freedman to the Defense Department, which said such information could not be released without the permission of Freedman's family, the *Tribune-Review* said.

CHAPTER 9

What Cannot Be Cured

"What cannot be cured, must be endured."

—Jewish proverb

AS I'VE MENTIONED, LUBBOCK HAS A POPULATION of over two hundred fifty thousand people, which includes fewer than one hundred Jews (a tiny fraction of the population). As a result, as one of the few Jewish mental health professionals around, it was a surprise to me when I was consulted to work with a Jewish family at the local hospital. However, this was no ordinary Jewish family. Rather, they were from Jerusalem in search of a cure for a rare condition for one of their children.

The father was an ultra-Orthodox rabbi with the bearing of religious royalty, Rabbi Avigdor Brazil. He was the real deal. He wore the traditional all-black suit, white shirt with no tie, black skullcap, and black shoes and socks. The rabbi looked like he stepped out of the seventeenth century directly into, of all places, West Texas.

The rabbi had ten children and a pregnant wife, all living together in a large home donated by a generous local physician. "One accepts all the children God grants you," the rabbi proudly told me. However, his oldest child, Sarah—a beautiful, intelligent, and at times oppositional-defiant eighteen-year-old—had been stricken by a rare bone infection that threatened her with amputation of her right arm. The family had traveled to the Cleveland Clinic first in their quest for treatment only to be told that the specialist they needed was an MD who happened to be at the Texas Tech University Health Science Center in Lubbock. Without hesitation the family picked up again and moved on.

The attending physician, recognizing the importance of establishing a cultural communication to develop rapport, thought of me, and the referral was made.

Although I was raised in a Conservative Jewish home, I had virtually no contact with ultra-Orthodox Jews. While they cannot deny the authenticity of my Jewish roots, they would scoff at my limited observance of the 613 commandments in the Torah, falling well short of their standard. In fact, the rabbi and his family came close to, if had not achieved, observance of each and every legal mandate. For this reason, I approached this consultation with some trepidation.

Sarah had been ill for quite some time, and she was sick of being sick. By the time she arrived in Lubbock, she had had her fill of doctors, tests, nurses, hospital rooms, and so on, and started acting out. Compounding the family's problems with her were her threats to leave ultra-Orthodoxy and strike out on her own in the secular world, ironically to become a health professional.

The rabbi's main duties in Jerusalem involved advancing the education of post–high school age girls (ages eighteen to twenty) while keeping them in the spiritual fold. This, of course, was the next stage of Sarah's education. At this time Sarah was so fed up with her compromised circumstances she often voiced her ambivalence to her shocked parents.

One day Sarah went AWOL from the hospital. A frantic search went on for a few hours until Sarah was returned by a cowboy, in full regalia, in his pickup truck. We neither asked nor were told what went on during her time away, but the cultural exchange must have been fascinating.

My job was to reconcile the family conflicts or at least lessen them during Sarah's treatment. I questioned whether the rabbi would grant me the authority to work with his family because of my (to him) essentially nonreligious status. Partially out of desperation, he entrusted his family to me, and I began working with Sarah, both in the hospital and later as an outpatient.

During these sessions she vented all her frustrations and fully expressed her irresolution about remaining in her community. Unlike many of her peers, Sarah had an interest in going to college and eventually leading her own life. Of course, that would mean abandoning her spiritual roots because it would be impossible for her to maintain her obligation to her complete observance of the Torah in the world at large. For her parents and community, there seemed to be no room for compromise.

This rigidity was best exemplified by the rabbi's insistence that he teach me how to properly pray with my phylacteries. It was his mitzvah (blessed obligation) to instruct wayward Jews like myself in whatever time he had to embrace as many of the commandments as possible. I dutifully retrieved my Bar Mitzvah phylacteries, but in disgust he deemed my set as unkosher and not worthy of prayer. He took them away and disposed of them without asking, promising to replace them with a kosher set, which he ultimately did. I did not resist, nor do I regret or resent these actions. In his mind, he was only doing what was "fit," and for unselfish reasons he wanted me to get it right.

I related this story to Sarah, who was aghast at her father's chutzpah. I was much more tolerant than she at that time. I could see how important this exchange was to him so I let it pass, but the reader can see the rigidity of his thinking—as with fundamentalists of any religion, such as the evangelicals at the Air Force Academy in Colorado Springs.

A little later I had a chance to test this rigidity. One Saturday I took a frantic call from him telling me that Sarah was in crisis and I needed to get to the hospital ASAP. I couldn't resist reminding him that I was forbidden to ride on the Sabbath and that I couldn't get there until nightfall. He promptly granted me rabbinical dispensation to travel for an emergency and I went, but not without needling him a bit. (Of course, I would have gone anyway.)

One incident was particularly reflective of some unexpected flexibility. He told me in confidence that he would accept Sarah's decision to leave the fold and pursue a traditional career rather than see her miserable. His only requirement was that she marry a Jew. His love for his family transcended all else, which is in itself a Talmudic principle.

With this increasing tolerance in mind, I was able to work toward common ground, not only between him and his daughter, but between him and me as well. I could sense a growing tolerance for me as I continued working to assuage family conflicts. After all, I would not have been there to do what I did for them had I been raised in an ultra-Orthodox tradition. He knew it. I had earned the necessary credibility to do my job, which I thought I would never be granted—no small accomplishment. Perhaps having lived in Lubbock for several weeks, the rabbi had a new perspective. He spent a considerable amount of time in contact with the locals, Jews and Gentiles alike, and it is hard to imagine that the warm welcome he received did not contribute to his newfound empathy. In fact, when his wife delivered her eleventh child, a boy, he was promptly nicknamed "Tex."

One day near the end of the family's stay in Lubbock, the rabbi asked me how I could be so happy since I lived a life of relatively little religious observance. I told him that I loved my wife, family, work, friends, and where I lived, while never losing sight of who I am as a Jew. This answer seemed to satisfy him.

Only days before the family returned to Jerusalem, when Sarah's prognosis was still very guarded, the rabbi unexpectedly appeared at my office with a gift basket. It was Purim, and it is tradition to give a gift such as this in gratitude to a respected acquaintance. The rabbi without hesitation walked into a waiting room full of West Texans who looked at him in wonder. He then proudly presented me with this gift.

A few weeks later, the hospital received a faxed photograph of Sarah's intact forearm. There was no note attached.

In 2018 I called Rabbi Brazil in Jerusalem to obtain permission to use this anecdote. I also got to talk to Sarah, who informed me that she would be attending medical school in Israel. I didn't have to inquire as to whether she would remain religiously observant. I was totally confident in her ability to balance her life.

Like Sarah, Greg has always been a very well-balanced person, and I had complete confidence that he would continue to remain steady throughout his life, in spite of its complexity—which proved to be true. Rather than have his identity become another complicating issue it served to help successfully integrate all the other aspects of his life. This became especially important during the times of extreme frustration when Greg briefly indicated that the novel excitement of fighter pilot training was wearing off. Occasional reminders that his military career should be appreciated in the context of his entire life seemed to help effect and maintain the desired balance.

Many military heroes of the week had to depend on an Act of Congress to receive their medals. However, since significant social change has occurred, partially due to the efforts of people like Greg and his forebears, Jewish military veterans are getting the recognition they deserve without complication and in a timely fashion.

01/03/2006

Dear Greg,

It is a sad statement about racism and anti-Semitism that the aforementioned Defense Authorization Act had to be passed to give minorities their just due. Let's hope that these days are well behind us.

I've already told you about Tibor Rubin but I knew nothing of the other minority servicemen. It makes me wonder about how many others have been neglected by history. They probably wouldn't care much, but this (selflessness) is part of what makes them heroic.

I can't say that I'm surprised by the glow of the fighter pilot candidacy wearing off some. I have said in the past about your attributes which resemble those of your fellow pilots. However, there are a whole lot of things different about you than your Jewishness. I think that you will really enjoy civilian life and all its amenities, not that this will necessarily make you an inferior officer. It's just that your life will be balanced. You'll be able to enjoy the best of both worlds. Your family and career will come first and the Guard will fill in as a nice complement. There's absolutely nothing wrong with that.

The countdown has begun.

Love, Norm

Leonard Kravitz

Lenny Kravitz was called to action during the Korean War where he saved most of his platoon from Chinese attack. For his heroism he was posthumously awarded the Distinguished Service Cross. As with so many other Jews, Kravitz's receipt of the medal was suspected to be delayed by anti-Semitic attitudes of the time. Many years later, after a thorough review of the historical record in the US military, multiple delayed and posthumous medals were awarded. As Churchill stated, "Give the US time and it usually gets it right." Churchill was correct.

Rep. Robert Wexler, Democrat from Florida and supporter of the Leonard Kravitz Jewish War Veterans Act of 2001, stated, "There is absolutely no justification for discrimination of any kind when we honor America's heroes. I am hopeful that the Leonard Kravitz Jewish War Veterans Act of 2001 will finally recognize those Jewish veterans, like Leonard Kravitz, whose noble actions clearly warrant the recognition of the Congressional Medal of Honor." The MOH was awarded to Kravitz in 2012.

•

History—military and otherwise—is full of ironies, and I found an anecdote about the possibility of former allies fighting each other at the birth of the State of Israel too compelling to resist. From the ghettoes of Eastern Europe to the establishment of their own viable state, Jews at the time rose above all odds to ensure their continuing existence. Their military skills, which kept them alive, were well utilized in keeping their nation alive. This evolution of identity and character could only be useful for Greg's quest.

This week's figure was a character in every sense of the word. He showed the same fighting spirit as the early Israelis. Some of his fighting was off the battlefield, such as the time he knocked out a Russian diplomat in a New York City restaurant after hearing him spouting anti-Semitic slurs. Sam would have found a home in the Israeli military had the timing been right.

Greg and I eventually did make it to the Slaton Air Museum in Slaton, Texas. One of the exhibits at the museum was an old book that was opened to a picture of Lt. Robert Stanford Tuck. I thought it was quite providential at the time.

01/09/2006

Dear Greg,

I keep telling you about this air museum in Slaton and we never seem to make it. Now that they are expanding yet again we definitely need to see it. For a private group they have put together a fairly impressive collection, as eclectic as it is.

My recent research has uncovered more historical ironies of Jewish military history. For example while reading the book about the partisans in the forests of Russia and Poland I discovered that many of them made it to Israel and became the backbone of the Israeli Defense Force. These people evolved from cowering ghetto-mentality Jews to an effective guerilla force to the foundation of one of the most powerful armed services (per capita) in the world. Remember this all happened in the space of about 4-5 years.

Anyway, the two ironies, which caught my eye, were the following. First, among the earliest of the aircraft comprising the fledgling Israeli Air Force were four Messerschmitts which were brought for scrap before the War of Independence (1948). The other irony occurred at the close of said war in 1949 when the Israelis overstepped their boundaries and went into Egyptian territory. To get them to turn back the Egyptians sent six of their early British

jets to intimidate the Israelis. All were
shot down without any Jewish losses.

I guess you are about 15 weeks away from
graduation. It really doesn't seem all that
long to wait and it will pass quickly. May
the spirit of guys like Sam Dreben carry
you with relative ease the rest of the way
and well beyond.

Love, Norm

Sam Dreben

Today's hero was recommended by Cousin Byron a long time ago,
but I never read anything about him until Byron sent me his biogra-
phy. If anyone broke the stereotype of Jewish cowardice, Sam Dreben
did. This guy would rather fight than breathe, and fight he did in
Nicaragua, Honduras, Mexico, and the Philippines, and in Europe
during World War I where he received high medals from the French
and Belgians as well as the Americans.

He was a born warrior—one of those guys who dries up and blows
away without a war to fight. I think this is exactly what happened to him.

Some warriors are made by the circumstances in which they find
themselves. Others are born, like Dreben. Dreben was the youngest of
five brothers, the other four of whom attended rabbinical school. Sam
would have none of it and was attracted to a life in the military.

After immigrating to the United States from Russia at age eighteen,
Sam enlisted in the Army and began a remarkable career. He fought
in the Spanish–American War (1899) in the Philippines and helped
rescue Westerners during the Boxer Rebellion in China (1901) before
leaving the service in 1902.

After finding civilian life unsatisfying, he reenlisted in 1904 and
became extremely proficient with the newly developed machine gun.

After his discharge in 1907, Sam was recruited by various liberation movements in Central America and Mexico.

Dreben later fought with and against Francisco Madera and Pancho Villa during the Mexican Revolution. Following the infamous raid on Columbus, New Mexico, that killed several American civilians, Dreben joined Gen. John "Black Jack" Pershing on a punitive but ultimately unsuccessful expedition.

At the ripe age of thirty-nine, Dreben reenlisted in the Army for a third tour of duty in 1917. He was subsequently sent to France where he was awarded the Distinguished Service Cross, the Croix de Guerre, and the Médaille militaire, France's entirely military active highest commendation. Gen. Pershing, who had been given command of the American Expeditionary Forces, regarded him as the finest soldier and one of the bravest men he ever knew. In confirmation, Dreben was quoted as saying, "I hear the captain say 'Forward!' and I don't hear nobody say 'Stop.'"

•

Greg's career outside of the military is in banking, so with this next letter I was able to combine his two major interests. The irony in this story is that the same Jews who had been disparaged as weak and cowardly were prevented from fighting until they were needed. Once they did fight, they quickly dispelled the stereotype, which was no surprise to Major de Rothschild, this week's hero.

The Jewish experience in the history of Great Britain can be summed up in a quote from the Oscar-winning movie *Chariots of Fire*. In the movie, two members of England's 1924 Olympic track team, one Christian and one Jew, are discussing what it is like to be a Jew in Great Britain. The Jew states, "They lead us to water but won't let us drink." Since the late nineteenth century, the British had been sending mixed messages about a Jewish homeland; this quote is just another example of British ambivalence about the Jews.

Dear Greg,

I think that we talked about this subject before so forgive me if I repeat myself. Hundreds of Jews already living in Palestine in the '40s wanted a shot at the Germans and chomped at the bit while the British, who controlled Palestine at the time, held them in check. The Brits' worst nightmare was that the Jews would get trained to fight the Germans and then take the training back to Palestine to be used against them.

Of course this is exactly what happened. They learned their lessons well and used them to gain independence from the Brits and the Arabs. What people don't know is that before WWII ended the Brits finally relented and set what came to be known as the "Jewish Brigade" loose. After three years of frustration they accounted for themselves very well. It's interesting that the British Army assigned a Jewish senior officer to the ragtag band of Jewish volunteers.

I wonder what happened to him. In line with the possible historical ironies posed last week, perhaps Rothschild later fought against the very men he trained after Israeli independence was declared. I found these ironies painful and prideful at the same time. While these historical para-doxes are not unique to Jews, the drama in

the ones which do exist are profound to say
the least. I pray that nothing about your
military career will be in the same vein.

Love, Norm

Edmund Leopold de Rothschild

Near the end of World War II, in April 1945, Major de Rothschild led Britain's Jewish Brigade against seasoned German troops and won an important battle in Italy. Palestinian Jews were finally let loose to fight the Germans after years of being stifled.

•

Although I was swelling with pride about Greg's military commitment and obligation, many others—family and friends alike—saw it very differently. Until I learned not to expect much from people, every time I was responded to less than enthusiastically, it grated on me deeply. Greg was caught between two camps, each claiming that what he was doing was "not Jewish." Some anti-Semites think Jews are duty shirkers, while others see military service as "not Jewish"—very frustrating as it appeared that there was no winning either way.

Greg handled these interactions much more graciously than I did, but they did bother him. He learned that some life decisions, no matter how awesome the accomplishment, will go unappreciated and even denigrated.

I suppose this was a good lesson for him to learn as a young man. He knows what he did and what the larger ramifications of his success might be, so this is more than enough.

The reference below is to Gen. John J. Pershing and a statement he made during World War I that disparaged the fighting ability of Jews under his command.

01/23/2006

Dear Greg,

I am very irked at the people who are lukewarm at best about your accomplishments. I will give you the same advice I give myself, i.e., do not have any expectations whatsoever of enthusiasm from them and avoid the subject unless they bring it up. This is a polite way of agreeing to disagree about values and it will be a lot less frustrating in the long run.

They have no concept of the difficulty and significance of what you are doing. They won't get it later either so save yourself some frustration. Of course this doesn't mean that you are loved any less; it simply means that regarding the military, you are on different planets.

The issue of Jewish volunteerism is particularly irksome. Most Jews by an overwhelming number volunteered for duty in all of America's wars. This trend is unlikely to change, but you should recognize your accomplishments from their uniqueness rather than as something "non-Jewish." Depend on those who "get it," at least partially, for your support.

Today's hero is a Jewish general, imagine that. I wonder if his family was embarrassed because he didn't become a doctor or go into law. Anyway, as you can see Gen. Frederick Knefler left a promising career in law.

```
    I think I've already sent you Pershing's
anti-Semitic quote. It is too bad we have
to be thought of separately from other
Americans. Whatever, embrace it and kick
butt while you do!
```
Love, Norm

Frederick Knefler

After fighting with the revolutionary forces in the Hungarian war of liberation in 1848–1849, Frederick Knefler emigrated to the United States and settled in Indiana. With the start of the Civil War twelve years later, Knefler was commissioned as a first lieutenant and quickly rose through the ranks.

Knefler made an impression on his superiors in several famous battles, including the Battles of Shiloh, Stones River, Chickamauga, and especially Missionary Ridge. At this last battle, Knefler received plaudits for leading a bold cavalry charge while displaying considerable gallantry, courage, and fidelity.

Later, Knefler fought in Tennessee and Georgia, where he played major roles in several important battles, including the Battles of Franklin and Nashville. For his achievements Knefler was promoted to brigadier general on March 13, 1865.

•

This next letter is a follow-up on the issue of Jewish apathy and a lack of appreciation for the military. The Vietnam War and the 1960s changed a lot of attitudes, Jewish ones included, and we are left with this unfortunate legacy to this day.

As a psychologist I am aware of the importance of fulfilling a passionate dream even if it doesn't make sense to others. Greg received a lot of support from many people over the years but at the same time has had to contend with very different viewpoints. The fact that he had this drive and interest in him since childhood should have been a factor in the judgment of others, but unfortunately it wasn't.

01/30/2006

Dear Greg,

I promise not to beat this subject to death but here is another piece describing Jewish volunteerism in a time of war. The 100+ Jews who served in the Revolutionary War did not have to join. I'm sure they joined for the same reasons all soldiers volunteer, both good and bad. The point is that they were there and no one can prove otherwise. The onus of proof should be on the anti-Semites to support their contentions of non-participation by Jews in times of war.

I agree with you that it is a bit disturbing to be underrepresented in the military, but that makes what you do that much more special. There will always be a few good (Jewish) men who will have the courage of their convictions as well as the courage to allow themselves to be who they are supposed to be. Anti-military Jews seem to forget that an interest in the military transcends politics and gravitates into the arena of personal fulfillment and self-actualization. Most of the critics of the Jewish military man forget about the

significance of passion and may have not
felt passionate about much, if anything.
  Anyway, keep up the good work for your
people, your country and yourself.

Love, Norm

Edward Salomon

Edward Salomon is the second Civil War general for the Union worthy of note. After the war began, Salomon joined the Illinois infantry as a second lieutenant. He quickly gained the attention of his superiors for his dedication, tactical excellence, intense patriotism, and bravery in actions. As a result, in 1862, he was promoted, to major.

Salomon was again promoted, to lieutenant colonel, after helping to organize a new combat regiment, the 82nd Illinois Infantry. The 82nd was unusual in that it comprised Jewish and other Eastern European immigrant volunteers. As a commander of the 82nd at the Battle of Gettysburg, Salomon was reported to have displayed the highest order of cool and determination under trying circumstances. His corps commander, Gen. Carl Schurz, described him as "the only soldier at Gettysburg who did not dodge when Lee's guns thundered."

CHAPTER 10

Whoever Saves a Soul

"Whoever destroys one soul destroys the entire world, and whoever saves a soul saves the entire world."

—Jewish proverb

AT SEVERAL TIMES THROUGHOUT GREG'S LIFE, I tried to find opportunities to help deepen his connection to flying. On one occasion I arranged for a tour of the Slaton Air Museum in Slaton, Texas. As mentioned earlier, this display is relatively unique in that it is private, supported by the efforts of one impassioned flight enthusiast who was able to assemble an impressive variety of vintage aircrafts. Slaton is a very small town about twenty minutes from Lubbock.

The curator met us and gave us our own tour of the grounds, which were crammed with aircraft history. We had a blast. After completing the tour we were led inside to a large room that served as a would-be museum. We were walking in the aisles viewing a wide assortment of flight memorabilia when I stopped dead in my tracks.

In a glass case was a book opened to a picture and story of none other than Flt. Lt. Robert Tuck, the one character I used as a symbol of the quintessential Jewish fighter pilot. Coincidences like these seemed to pop up throughout the course of our journey over the years.

During the Holocaust, one of the darkest periods in Jewish history, survivors provide living testimony. Their experiences are no doubt difficult to hear, but in spite of everything, we can learn from their resilience.

I have met many Holocaust survivors, but one in particular stands out. Her name was Helene Shiver. Shortly after I moved to Lubbock and joined the local synagogue, I had the pleasure of meeting her. She was born into a well-to-do family in Sofia, Bulgaria, and was living a life of privilege until 1941 when the Nazis invaded and seized control of the country. Then they came after the Jews.

Helene was the only survivor from her entire family. Her relative youth and attractiveness saved her. I remember hearing her moving and powerful story at the synagogue. She brought the Holocaust to life with her family photos and vivid memories. Her therapist had strongly advised her to speak to as many houses of faith and civic groups as possible to help purge her grief. Although it took years to heed the doctor's advice, she eventually complied and told her story repeatedly. However, she never ran out of tears. She never elaborated on her experiences in painful detail, but one could put together enough pieces to admire her bravery and will to survive.

My vivid memories are of her and Greg together at the synagogue. Helene had a sweet way around all children, and Greg was no exception. I remember, during his childhood and adolescence, her gently touching his cheek and praising any virtue or accomplishment she found out about, no matter how small. She did this with every Jewish child she met. They were precious to her because she was witness to an organized effort to eliminate the entirety of Jewish youth. Each young life was a statement that there would be a Jewish future. In fact,

Helene was taken when she in the eighth grade, celebrating a birthday party at home with her family. When the Nazis burst through
the door, the butler told them to leave. She watched as he was fatally
shot in front of her. Little did she know that was just the beginning
of the atrocities she would witness. Just a few minutes later, her uncle
would be shot trying to retrieve his sleeping child, David, from the
second floor. Seconds later, the upstairs maid and the baby were shot
as well. Helene stood frozen with her mother, who motioned for her
not to speak.

For three hellish weeks, she and her family, along with more
than one hundred others, were packed into a railcar and herded like
livestock to the concentration camp. Once there, she hid her only
worldly possessions, two small pictures of her parents, in her boots.
Everything else was taken away, including most of her teeth. Later, she
was tattooed with her number D2832. The D was for the concentration camp's name, Dachau.

While incarcerated in Dachau, she and the other female members of
her family were made to do despicable, horrid jobs, including making
lampshades from human skin. Over the course of three years, one by
one the female members of Helene's family died. The male members
she never again saw after they were separated upon their arrival at
the camp. Her mother was the last to die, but on her way to the gas
chamber, she blew Helene a kiss and implored her, "Tell them!" At the
time, Helene didn't know what her mother meant. Later in her life,
she knew and vowed to tell anyone who could listen about what was
done to her and millions of others, simply because they were Jewish.
She always knew that her strength and courage came from God and
credited him for keeping her alive.

After she married one of the American soldiers who helped liberate
Dachau, her mother-in-law encouraged her to have the hateful tattoo
removed, because questions about it continued to upset Helene. I
met another survivor who kept his tattoo as a symbol of defiance and
survival. Whatever their choices, whatever their decisions, it seems

that each one found a way to keep memories of this unspeakable chapter in Jewish history alive.

In 1975, I had an even more personal encounter with living Jewish history. In response to repeated requests over the years from my aging father, he and I returned to the family roots in Bialystok, Poland. My father, his eight brothers and sisters, and his parents immigrated a few at a time in the early 1900s. They were refugees escaping murderous anti-Semitic pogroms instigated by the czarist government to distract the Russian and Polish people from their common misery.

On this trip I first became aware of what it means to be a Jew. It was also my first and worst experience of being the object of intense anti-Semitism. My expectations for the trip were to learn more about the details of life in the Pale of Settlement and also to spend some long-delayed quality time with my father.

Near the end of our two weeks in Poland, we were allowed to leave the guided tour for three days and see Bialystok on our own. (Because Poland was still in the Soviet sphere, travel without approved guides was limited.) The town had been rebuilt, and most of prewar Jewish life had been erased.

I thought I might learn more about the family history at the Jewish cemetery. However, every—and I mean every—single gravestone had been removed by the Nazis and used as paving blocks in roads. We did find the site of the synagogue my family attended, but instead of a viable house of worship we found a monument to the hundreds of Jews who were packed into the building and burned alive.

Out of a prewar population of twenty thousand Jews—one-tenth the size of Bialystok's population—only fifteen remained. Not fifteen thousand or fifteen hundred: fifteen! My father's fluency in Yiddish came in handy as we gathered three of the remaining Jews and took them to dinner. After a raucous meal we stood outside of the restaurant to say good-bye when it happened.

Gradually, a crowd of teens and young adults formed around us and began hurling insults and anti-Semitic epithets. Our presence alone was enough to provoke the raging hatred that had been instilled in Poland's youth from their earliest days.

The men around me, including my father, were quite unbothered by their tormentors. It was almost as if they expected this to happen and were therefore inured to the actual event. The group said their good-byes and went their separate ways without a word being said about what had just happened.

To say the least, after this incident and our visit to Auschwitz, my identity was shaken. I felt I needed to do something in response to the past and, yes, current threat to my people.

Upon our return I vowed to affirm my identity by never eating pork or shellfish again, a pledge by which I've abided. More importantly, I promised myself to raise at least one child with a strong Jewish identity.

•

The story in this next letter was Greg's favorite of all the documented and anecdotal histories that I found in the year of research I conducted. Hermann Goering's respect and admiration for his former flightmate's courage and flying skills transcended the Nazi leader's anti-Semitism when this Jewish World War I pilot intervened to save the life of a fellow pilot, Fritz Beckhardt. Goering's affinity for Air Force personnel regardless of nationality or religion was the reason POW camps for downed airmen provided better conditions than did camps for army POWs. It is reasonable to speculate that he may have had a hand in preventing the wanton slaughter of Jewish prisoners at the war's end.

Pilot camaraderie, especially that of fighter pilots, is incomparable for its loyalty and dedication. This fact in and of itself has been a great source of comfort for parents of a son who aspire to such a dangerous vocation. Whenever Greg flies we leave him in the best of hands.

02/03/2006

Dear Greg,

I can't tell you how pleased I am about Gen. Newman's interest in you. I think that you will agree that he is very sincere and the Jewish connection only will make your relationship with him even more special.

Pilots do have a powerful bond but never was it tested as much as it was by today's hero, Willy Rosenstein. He was a fine pilot but an even better friend.

As the Nazis began rising in power and the Jewish persecutions intensified, even loyal Jews, who were in the military during WWI, were victimized. Fritz Beckhardt, a Jewish WWI ace I wrote to you about, somehow got in trouble with the Nazis and got thrown in jail. As you know it was only a short trip between there and the work/death camps. (Beckhardt was the guy who flew to Switzerland rather than turn in his plane after WW I.)

Anyway, Rosenstein gets wind of his buddy Beckhardt's predicament and appeals to, of all people, Hermann Goering, with whom he flew in WWI. Believe it or not, Goering arranges for Beckhardt's release in spite of the antipathy he felt toward Rosenstein in particular and Jews in general. Blood is thicker than water and pilot blood is much thicker than regular blood.

So enjoy your camaraderie with pilots new and old for there seems to be nothing like it.

Love, Norm

02/10/2006

Dear Greg,

I really appreciated the letter you sent Gen. Newman. You couldn't have worded it any better. A man with his accomplishments and stature has every reason to feel good about what he has done with his life especially at this late stage. I like the modesty of the WWII vets—but they deserve all the credit they can get. Of course, as a Jew, his considerable achievements and outstanding career make what he did that much sweeter. Definitely, get him to tell you some of his stories. You will appreciate them more than I can and from his perspective you make for a better audience. (He was pleasantly surprised when I told him Tuck was a Jew because he knew all about his reputation but not his background.) I really hope that Gen. Newman can come to the graduation. He can add so much to the proceedings. (I already know that Tuck wouldn't miss it for the world and will be there in spirit.)

Love, Norm

During the celebration that followed the wings ceremony one of Greg's flight mates and I got into a discussion of what constitutes "cool" in a pilot. He provided a relatively conventional definition, that is, performing with aplomb under pressure, not breaking a sweat, and looking good to women while doing so. Having the benefit of historical perspective drawn from this narrative, I had a somewhat different definition. It went as follows: maintaining complete control and composure while knowing that one's people were being destroyed below, and being prepared to do so for the duration.

Jeff Gurvitz

Jeff Gurvitz was killed in Vietnam in 1968 while trying to save the life of a fellow soldier during a mortar attack. He left the relative safety of a foxhole in a selfless act that cost him his own life. Gurvitz was awarded a Bronze Star for his bravery.

His wife, Barbara Sonneborn, although she remarried and took up photography as a profession, mourned his death for twenty years before she was inspired to write letters to her deceased husband in order to resolve her grief.

The approach worked. The power of letters to heal effectively allowed Jeff's wife to finally gain closure on her tragic loss and move on to help others find peace.

02/17/2006

Dear Greg,

I wasn't going to include Haym Salomon on the list of heroes because I thought he was just a financier, not that this wasn't important at the time. Financing is what Jews do anyway so I didn't want to reinforce the stereotype myself. However, I didn't realize that Salomon was tortured and condemned to be hanged because of his revolutionary activities. In addition, had we lost the war he most certainly would have been ruined financially by the British so his risks were considerable. I also appreciate the fact that love of country was an aspect of Judaism, something you may be discovering as your military career progresses. Anyway, Haym richly deserves to be included.

Doing this research has given me perspective on the definition of cool: getting into your plane, flying unlimited sorties in the fight to save Western Civilization knowing that your people are being helplessly slaughtered beneath you, while also knowing that you are up against some of the most experienced pilots who ever flew and then landing and getting out of your plane looking like you stepped off the cover of *GQ*. To me, cool is best represented by pilots like Tuck who unfortunately may never be appreciated as much as he should be.

Pardon my rant.

Much love, Norm

Haym Salomon

Haym Salomon sympathized with the patriotic cause during the Revolutionary War soon after immigrating to the United States. In 1776 he was arrested as a spy and tortured by the British during his eighteen months of captivity. The British pardoned him from his sentence early so that they could use him as an interpreter for Hessian troops.

While in the role of interpreter, Salomon used his position to help American prisoners of war escape captivity and encouraged the Hessians to desert. In 1778 he was arrested for the second time and sentenced to death. However, he managed to escape and lived to see America's independence actualized.

•

Introduction to Fighter Fundamentals (IFF) is an intermediate pilot training program between Undergraduate Pilot Training (UPT) and training in Greg's designated aircraft, the F-16. It was a difficult ten weeks, which he ultimately survived hopefully with a little help from the ubiquitous Lt. Tuck. This will make more sense when you read the last letter.

Greg is not as big a baseball fan as I am, but he knows who this week's personality was and what he stood for as an American and as a Jew. That is plenty enough for me.

02/23/2006

Dear Greg,

As big a baseball fan as I've been I never knew about Hank Greenberg's war record. Even though he was at the time the highest-paid player in the majors and could have returned to play in 1941, after fulfilling his military obligation, he immediately volunteered after Pearl Harbor to stay in the Army. Then he went on to become a captain with the Army Air Corps in a combat zone. Maybe it will take another Pearl Harbor-like incident to get Jews more involved in the

military but wasn't 9/11 enough? Greenberg
is worthy of hero status on two counts.

I know that you are concerned about
Introduction to Fighter Fundamentals but
in the same way I knew ahead of time that
you would get this far, I know that you
will make it all the way. All you have
to remember is to just get back to the
150th. That's pressure enough to ensure
your success. You don't have to do any more
than that. Whatever challenges IFF throws
at you I'm sure that you can handle them
the way you managed the tough early months
of Undergraduate Pilot Training.

The prize is now a year closer. In the
process of getting there I am pleased that
you are the same Greg now that you were at
the onset of training, while remembering
who you are.

Love, Norm

Hank Greenberg

Hank Greenberg's distinguished baseball career was interrupted in
1940 when he was drafted into the US Army. Three months later he
was discharged when Congress decided that men over twenty-eight
years old did not have to serve. However, after Pearl Harbor, Greenberg
reenlisted out of a sense of patriotism and duty. Rather than serve in
the safe capacity of athletic instructor, Greenberg chose to serve in the
Army Air Corps in the China-Burma-India Theater, where he distinguished himself.

•

There comes a time in the life of every parent of a child who will be thrust in harm's way to consider mortality in the context of life and its purpose. Greg's mother and I are no exceptions, but it gave us great comfort to know that, more likely than not, his fearsome skills would be used to try to make the world a better place and save American and others' lives along the way. I am proud and confident to say that he has done both.

I thought that at this phase of his training a change in the tenor of these letters should occur. Greg has never been one to shy away from the consideration and consequences of death. The next three letters I wrote emphasize the impact death has on families when a loved one dies in combat. I knew that he would appreciate and be enriched by the survivors' sentiments.

The letters referred to from Stephan Cohan's daughter and Jeff Gurvitz's wife are copyrighted and therefore are not reproduced here. Greg read them, though, and was deeply moved.

03/01/2006

Dear Greg,

Since you are approaching the completion of your training, I thought that it is time to change the tone of these letters a bit. A glass is broken at a Jewish wedding partially to remind us that even during a time of celebration we are compelled to remember that the world is still "broken" and that we have work to do within our own individual abilities to make it whole. I hope that you will be used as a pilot toward

that end, and if you are, your service to
your country will be well worth whatever
frustrations you periodically endure.

In keeping with the broken glass tradition, I am including with your next three
letters the names and stories of two Jewish
boys who gave their lives in hopes of trying
to make the world a better place. I think
you understand that I'm not trying to be
morbid. However, I do think that it is good
for all of us to consider our mortality and
that during our time on earth we shouldn't
take it for granted and do our best to
fulfill our purpose for being here.

I hope you appreciate them and make your
life more meaningful.

Much love, Norm

CHAPTER 11

A Rule of Caution

"A basic rule of caution: Don't be overly cautious."

—Jewish proverb

WHILE I WAS SEARCHING OUT JEWISH MILITARY heroes, some delightful surprises took place along the way. One of my most memorable discoveries was of the wartime memoirs of the now-deceased Dr. Jerry Jacobs. My sister Linda had been friends with Jacobs and his wife, Shirley, but due to his modesty, Linda knew little of his military exploits in World War II. When my sister learned of this project, she thought his widow would prove to be an excellent resource. Mrs. Jacobs was entirely open to my research, and she readily provided a copy of her husband's memoirs, which he did not complete until 1998, shortly before his death.

Jacobs's narrative fit the theme of this book perfectly. In it he described dogfights in harrowing detail during which he shot down three German fighters before being shot down himself. Later, he spent several months in a POW camp, which he also vividly described, before being liberated in May 1945.

Dr. Jacobs's story represents the anonymity of so many of his peers who deserve to be remembered for what they quietly did to honor their country and their people. What follows is an excerpt from his memoir that typifies the courage, resolve, and tenacity of his comrades:

> We had just arrived over the battle area when the ground control, using radar, vectored us toward a large enemy fighter force heading toward the battle area. Before long we were in the midst of a whirling air battle with German Messerschmitt 109s and Focke Wolfe [*sic*] 190s. This was it! My first encounter with the enemy. I was able to immediately recognize the ME109s and the FW190s and the thing that really made my eyes bulge was seeing the big iron cross insignia on their aircraft. I couldn't believe that I was now face-to-face with someone who was going to try to kill me. My brain automatically shifted gears going from standby to full alert. This was for real and I felt that I was ready. I had no feeling of fear, or anger, but one of great excitement. As I look back I realized that I was cool and there was no panic; just a job to do. All of my senses were on alert. It was my job now to get one of the enemy in my gunsight and destroy him. I knew that it was the enemy who was here for the same reason, to destroy me. (Jacobs, 1998)

While conducting background research on this project, I learned that Jacobs was directly connected to two unique events in the Jewish military experience in World War II. First, it was unique to Jews as POWs to live with the daily fear of execution for simply being Jewish. By the time he was shot down and captured in September 1944, the Holocaust was well known to most if not all Jewish servicemen. They were aware that, if captured, they would be relegated to a special category.

In fact, in some POW camps Jews were segregated from their Christian peers with their fate left uncertain. That threat to Jewish personnel was significant enough that many were issued two sets of dog tags, one indicating Protestant (P) and the other Hebrew (H). Jacobs was not in one of the camps where Jews were segregated, so at a routine roll call when his fellow POWs were asked to reveal his religion, he panicked.

Fortunately, rather than simply pull the tags out and discovering the religion himself, the camp's officer conducting the inquiry took the word of the POW. By this time Jacobs had established a friendship with a Christian POW who helped him be knowledgeable with the basics of Christianity. When the inquisition reached him, Jacobs firmly blurted out, "Protestant!" The officer went on to the next in line and Jacobs breathed a deep sigh of relief, "Praise Jesus."

The second interesting historical event of which Jacobs was a part had to do with an order sent down from the German High Command that all Jewish POWs were to be segregated (if they weren't already) and executed so that they would not be able to be liberated. For some unknown reason the order was never carried out.

Rather, Jacobs and thousands of other Army Air Corps POWs were gathered from several camps and taken on a long forced march in horrible winter conditions. Their German captors were trying to avoid capture by the rapidly advancing Russians, but they also may have been trying to preemptively curry favor with the Western Allies. In any event, Jacobs survived the march and was liberated in May 1945, bent but not broken.

03/08/2006

Dear Greg,

Happy Anniversary to all of us! I can't believe I've known you for 20 years and I couldn't have asked for a more complete life. Sometimes people look at me askance when they hear Carol's and my story, particularly about my decision not to have children. They seem to think that there is something inherently superior of biological

over "adopted" children. I beg to differ. No
one can diminish the pleasure and reward I
have received from having raised you. The
joy of helping you get where you want to
be one day is something I look forward to
being a part of. Beyond that maybe we can
sit back for a while and simply reflect
with satisfaction for a life well lived.

I was touched by the letter from Jeff
Gurvitz's wife. Gurvitz was a real hero
which she acknowledged and won't forget
but he was her husband first and foremost
however brief. I think that most of us want
to be remembered with the love she has
for Jeff. General Newman's statement about
being fearful of dying with no one to say
Kaddish for him sticks with me. May we all
be remembered.

Love, Norm

Whenever I had the opportunity, I sent Greg evidence of Jewish volunteerism as another means of lessening his isolation. The poignancy of these
stories was profound, and I think had the intended impact. Recognizing
that I did not have many examples of female volunteers, I found the amazing story of a Russian Jewish woman who served in World War II.

03/14/2006

Dear Greg,

I have been remiss in not acknowledging
the significant contributions of Jewish

women to the war effort. This is a very much underappreciated aspect of the history of women in war in general and Jewish women specifically. Much as your grand-mother, Opal, who was among the first U.S. Navy Waves to volunteer in 1943 during WWII, Lydia Litvyak also volunteered for the Russians. Lydia, a Russian Jew, was an awesome combat pilot, who shot down eleven Nazi warplanes.

Love, Norm

P.S. Happy 20th Anniversary of our fate-ful meeting!

Lydia Litvyak

Desperate times call for desperate measures. With the Nazis attempting to overwhelm the Soviet Union and seize their eastern empire, a personnel shortage and a call for patriotism brought Lydia Litvyak into the war.

Lydia accounted for herself on the Eastern Front as "a born fighter pilot." Much to the humiliation of her German counterparts, Lydia proceeded to down an estimated eleven German airplanes, in the process enduring two forced landings and suffering injuries for which she refused medical leave. She became known as the "White Lily of Stalingrad" in Soviet press releases and the "White Rose of Stalingrad" in North America and European reports. During her career as a pilot she was awarded the Order of Lenin, the Order of the Red Banner, the Order of the Red Star, and the Order of the Patriotic War first class.

Lydia eventually was shot down in 1943. Unable to provide a body from the crash, Joseph Stalin refused to award her the Hero of the Soviet Union. It was not until 1990 that Mikhail Gorbachev awarded Lydia Litvyak the Hero of the Soviet Union and promoted her to the rank of senior lieutenant.

If there was ever a woman who defied the stereotype of Jewish princess, it was the indomitable, rebellious, and intrepid Lydia Litvyak.

•

At this point in the project I was starting to feel withdrawal symptoms knowing that our journey would end soon. I did not see this reaction coming. Because of the significance of knowing these histories and the opportunity the letters gave us to know each other better, a part of me didn't want it to end. Unique experiences like this cannot be duplicated, so as the end approached, I was relieved, grateful, and fulfilled but felt empty at the same time. I honestly wondered if we would have other experiences to bond and affirm our love for each other while helping us define ourselves at the same time.

I couldn't think of a more fitting hero to include in the series than this next pilot. Again, the timing of his heroism during World War II made this an especially fitting choice. To win Britain's highest medal at the most crucial time in its modern history makes him a hero among heroes. Someday it might be especially meaningful to travel to England and see the burial sites and monuments to pilots like Tuck and Aaron. Their contributions were immeasurable and should be honored forever.

3/22/2006

Dear Greg,

Since we are coming down to the wire, I didn't think that I would find such a gem as Arthur Louis Aaron. I passed over his name when reading about Tuck and I didn't think of him again until recently when I reread the Tuck piece and it finally stuck. Tuck received more medals but Aaron was more decorated in that he was awarded the Victoria Cross, which is Great Britain's Medal of Honor.

I was very moved by Aaron's heroics, so much so that I sent a more detailed description of his exploits. You told me how difficult it was to win the highest medal in air combat. There are probably very few in history (remember John Levitow in Vietnam?) and therefore Aaron's accomplishment is that much more significant. I don't see how there could be any greater act of courage and it is especially sweet that the Brits gave this honor to a Jew.

I will miss writing these letters at least if not more than you seem to have enjoyed them. It would be easy to keep doing this throughout your entire training but I wanted UPT to stand on its own since it was so difficult. It should get easier (and more fun) from here to F-16 qualification, but that doesn't mean that occasionally you won't get a "spiritual booster shot."

Much love, Norm

Arthur Louis Aaron

The Victoria Cross (VC) is an equivalent to the Medal of Honor in that it is awarded to those who exhibit a full measure of devotion to their brothers-in-arms, to those they are sworn to protect and to their country. This story of remarkable heroism is one of my favorites because it exemplifies this standard to a T. It reminds me of the John Levitow feat in that both men willingly sacrificed their lives for their crews under the most extreme circumstances. Aaron had already been awarded a Distinguished Flying Medal when he performed the deeds for which he was awarded the VC.

Aaron's citation reads,

> On the night of 12th August, 1943, Flight-Sergeant Aaron was captain and pilot of a bomber detailed to attack Turin. When approaching its target, the aircraft was hit by fire from an enemy fighter, which caused it to become unstable and difficult to control. Flight-Sergeant Aaron was wounded in the face and lung, and his right arm was rendered useless. After a rest, he made determined efforts to take control again—persuaded to desist, he wrote instructions with his left hand, and guided the bomb-aimer in the hazardous task of landing the damaged aircraft at Bone [Algeria] in North Africa.

Nine hours after landing, he died of exhaustion. "In appalling conditions he showed the greatest qualities of courage, determination and leadership, and though wounded and dying, he set an example of devotion to duty which has seldom been equaled and never surpassed." A scholarship to the Leeds School of Architecture was established in Aaron's memory, and in 2001 a statue of him was erected on the Eastgate Roundabout in Leeds. His parents donated his VC medal to the Leeds City Museum.

A Little Child, a Big Child

"A little child weighs on your knee, a big one on your heart."

—Jewish proverb

WHILE SOMEWHAT STRICT AS PARENTS, CAROL AND I appreciated the value of being flexible too. At several notable moments we permitted exceptions to the rules in order to send a message about prioritizing values.

For example, Greg was allowed to miss school when his childhood dog died. He spent the day digging a proper grave and mourning his first love.

Greg missed another school day when I moved my practice from its initial location to a more high-pressure setting. I was nervous, and he knew it. I became even more anxious when the one person who was supposed to help me move failed to appear. Without notice Greg showed up and helped mostly by calming my nerves.

A third example is particularly revealing of his character. A member of the local Jewish congregation and a career Air Force veteran had been hospitalized with terminal cancer. Greg had a relationship with him, as he always seemed to have with other veterans from the synagogue who weren't averse to telling their stories.

Anyway, I was making rounds one morning and decided to visit the individual. When I walked in the room during school hours Greg was sitting at his bedside listening intently. Not a word was said about Greg's cutting class that day. A few days later the man died.

Years later, while off duty, Greg chose to stay with the wounded at the Balad AFB Hospital in Iraq during his tour of duty.

Greg married a Jewish woman in 2005 who gave birth to their two children, Abby in 2009 and Sam in 2010. They are both receiving a Jewish education in Albuquerque, New Mexico, at Congregation Albert. Now that I am a grandfather, nicknamed "Normie," I still feel the same sense of obligation to pass on to my grandchildren what I gave to Greg. When he was nine years old, Sam asked me what I was most proud of in my life. I told him the following story.

Late one night a battered woman was brought to me in the Concord Hospital emergency room for crisis treatment. In the course of the interview, I learned that she lived only a few houses away from me on a lake in the woods where I bought my dream home. After settling her down and making my recommendation for her to continue to get help escaping from her husband, we went our separate ways.

A few weeks later I heard a loud rapping on my front door. There stood the same woman and her young daughter. Both were scared out of their minds. Her husband had gotten into a drunken rage, picked up a handgun, and shot it at his family; bullet holes were found later in the wall of her home. We did not know if her husband was coming after her to my house—armed and with the intent of inflicting further harm to his family.

Without thought or hesitation I immediately let the mother and daughter into my home and provided safety and comfort until the authorities arrived. Much later I considered this act in the context of Jewish history. Too many times over the centuries, the doors of countries (and neighbors) were closed to Jews who needed shelter from persecution. This family represented the oppressed and terrified who have few options. I'd like to think that I acted in concert with what others who shared these values did when Jews needed refuge. I consider this to be one of my finest moments.

•

Greg never forgot all those who helped him fulfill his dream, so when asked to give advice to other boys who might want to follow in his footsteps, he never hesitated. He has remained true to the character that earned him the ribbon for kindness in elementary school. For his mother and me this remains his most important award.

In regard to the listing of the heroes of the week, I intentionally left out their first names, not because they should be taken for granted, but rather perhaps someday the names of Jewish war heroes will be equitably acknowledged rather than regarded as glaring exceptions.

03/29/2006

Dear Greg,

Our journey is coming to an end. It has been exceptionally rewarding to see that these letters have been useful to you. This week's and next week's entries will bring this series to a conclusion. Sometimes it's rewarding to see a flurry of names (Jewish) together. It seems like an excla-mation point to the "argument" about the Jewish fighting man's willingness to fight and volunteer spirit. Remember, the names

I have given you are only a small fraction
of the overall contributions made—from the
bravest heroes to the lowliest grunts.

Assignment night is only two weeks away
and then the big day, certainly a beginning
and not an end, i.e., a true commencement.

I appreciate your interest and help with
those two boys who want to be fighter pilots.
Carol thinks I'm seeing pilot prospects
everywhere, but not really. I accept that
all the potential in the world won't make
them pilots automatically. However, I do see
the passion and drive which you had at age
7 and which should be encouraged in others.

That's it for now. Two to go.

Love, Norm

Abend, Shapiro, Krotoshinsky, Gumpertz, Hoffman, Katz, Samples, Frankl, Sonneborn, Goldstein, Jachman, Zussman, Foreman, Rosenstein, et al.

•

The next letter brings the series to a conclusion. It was written only days before Greg was awarded his wings at Vance. I never doubted that he would make the grade or get assigned to fighter training, for which only a fraction of the pilot candidates qualified. I was pleased and proud of him for not only accomplishing his difficult goal but for becoming an even better person as a result of his experiences.

Even at the end of this first training phase, I believed that it was important to continue to instill and strengthen his Jewish identity for the tough times that still lay ahead.

Metaphorically, I was comfortable leaving him in the care of the ubiquitous Lt. Robert Tuck, whom I have referenced as a figure of inspiration several times throughout this discourse. When in need of an emotional boost, all Greg had to do was glance over his shoulder and look for the wink and nod from his spiritual wingman.

In the same way that I knew that Greg would receive his wings, I also knew that he would someday earn his place among the pantheon of Jewish military personnel designated on the pyramid in the introduction. It may have seemed arrogant and disrespectful to include him so early in his career, but as far as I was concerned this journey was a done deal from the first time I became aware of his passion for flight. But his place in our people's history is well earned.

04/17/2006

Dear Greg,

Our long adventure in history comes to an end. It passed by in a flash as I'm sure the remainder of your training will, so take it all in and appreciate it, even the bad parts. The memories will be part of your collective past and I'm sure that you will treasure them someday in a similar way that many of my patients nearing the end of their lives do. No life should be defined by a few unpleasant events, which may even be useful in providing contrast to the vast majority of life-affirming experiences you will have.

I can't help but think that General Breedlove and General Newman frequently reflect on their lives in service to their country. The fact that both had brushes with death only made their lives that much sweeter. Being among the rare few who have the opportunity to fly fighters, as you will, has to be an especially satisfying and rewarding memory for them. How many people get to fulfill a life's dream, thoroughly enjoy the hell out of it and all that goes with it and serve your country at the same time? Please appreciate how special being one of a select few is now and into the future so that when it is your turn to stop and reflect upon your life, you will with no regrets.

I should like to think that the approximately 200 Jewish military heroes we have plucked from the annals of our collective past had that opportunity. Realistically, probably not, but the fact that they are remembered means that their contributions to our country and its freedoms will never die.

The definition of a hero is certainly a personal one. To me the fact that all the servicemen we reviewed embraced their Judaism, especially at times when it may have been more convenient not to, enhances their accomplishments. None of them wore their faith on their sleeves but they never denied it. And when it came time to decide how they would be buried and mourned many actively chose the Jewish way.

As we've discussed, history will not get in the way of destroying the stereotype of the Jew as a coward. Arguing against the stereotype only reinforces it. Being in the thick of it has always been the best way of proving ourselves as more than capable warriors as you are doing so ably. In the near future you will be in the spiritual company of these brave souls, not necessarily as a hero, but as a part of a long tradition.

Whenever you have a rough time in your service to your country, I guarantee that thinking about your predecessors and what they did to make what you did possible will make your challenge more than manageable. Let Flt. Lt. Tuck be your spiritual wingman and you should get through anything including IFF.

I cannot select a final Jewish Military Hero to conclude this series. Just as Jews throughout history have come together to survive, let our heroes be remembered collectively for what they did for our people, our nation and quite literally during WWII, the world. I have no doubt that they will welcome you as one of them now and forever.

With the greatest love, honor and
respect, Norm

CHAPTER 13

To Your Fellow

"That which is hateful to you do not do that to your fellow. That is the whole Torah, the rest is commentary, now go and learn it."

—Rabbi Hillel

BECAUSE OF MY CHOSEN PROFESSION, I CONVERSE with patients on average forty-plus hours per week. However, I have never been entirely comfortable with public speaking, even though I had conducted a considerable amount of training at a previous position. When I learned that my new job in Houston in 1988 would entail marketing via personal appearances, I became somewhat apprehensive. I wanted the job very badly in order to move closer to Carol and Greg, so I took it knowing that I would have to go into the community and speak to the advantages of sending teens to Weinberger & Associates for treatment.

I lost count of how many talks I gave, but for much of the next two years I worked for Weinberger, I recall giving one and occasionally two talks each week. I spoke to various civic organizations and health professional associations, but I most enjoyed talking to faith groups.

As I've indicated, I pretty much took my faith for granted, and I honestly didn't know a whole lot about other religions. Of course,

I had some exposure growing up close to Greek Orthodoxy, and in college I met and made good friends with the first fundamentalist Baptist I ever met. Yet I didn't know the tenets of other religions or their relationship to Judaism.

It was incumbent on me to learn more about Christianity if I was going to move to the Bible Belt. By then, since I was comfortable with my own faith, I was able to handle situations when asked about the Judeo-Christian divide. This ability became even more essential when I moved to Lubbock.

By that time, I came to believe in the importance of increasing even more my understanding of Judaism, especially in a part of the country where Jews were sparse. Word got around Lubbock that I would be willing to talk to moderate Christian churches of various denominations about the essentials of Judaism. Each time I did, I know that my spiritual identity strengthened. Not that I was challenged by those parishioners or anything like that, but more because I began appreciating what it took for Jews to historically survive in a veritable ocean of Christianity that was all too many times misunderstanding of Judaism.

Since I had a relatively strong Jewish education—that is, I could read Hebrew and was fairly well versed in Jewish history—I became more involved in the small local synagogue. At times there was no rabbi in residence, so I was asked to teach Hebrew in preparation for Bar and Bat Mitzvahs to several of the kids, Greg included. In addition, I was asked to teach the confirmation class, which was one of the most rewarding experiences of my life. I also was asked to assist at two funerals, a circumcision, and even a wedding.

At that time our most recent rabbi had prepared a curriculum from which I taught every Wednesday, the same night the Christian kids were receiving their religious instruction. Over five years I think I worked with about fifteen kids. I was well aware that without this instruction these children would have limited opportunity to develop their own spiritual identities.

When I told my extended Florida family what I was doing they were surprised, as I would have been prior to my move to Texas. My relatives had taken their identities and the state of Judaism in America for granted. After all, almost every other person with whom they spent their daily lives was Jewish. Being a tiny minority was out of the realm of their experience—something I hope they would think about and appreciate.

This readily came to life one day in Houston while I was writing up charts at the nursing station at Twelve Oaks Hospital, which houses an inpatient psychiatric unit for some of the area's most disturbed adolescents. I looked up and noticed that two other mental health professionals, one psychiatrist and one psychologist, were also charting.

Both were Jewish, one from South Africa and the other from Mexico. All three of our families were from proximate parts of the Pale of Settlement in Eastern Europe, an area where Jews were allowed to live but where basic rights such as attending school, joining guilds, and owning land were forbidden. They emigrated from their countries of origin by necessity and were accepted wherever they could find safety. We were "reunited" full circle in America, where we have common cause—an often-repeated story in Jewish history and one to never take for granted.

I wrote Greg one more letter as he struggled with intermediate training in the T-38. I thought he needed a morale boost at the time and tried to make the letter as authentic-looking and -sounding as possible. I also thought a laugh might do him good.

Given the historical circumstances at the time, recruitment letters such as these may very well have been sent to prospective volunteers: who knows? I'd like to think that Greg would have answered the call. Most fighter pilots regard the Battle of Britain as the ultimate test of one's air-to-air combat skills and wonder how they would have fared if given the chance. Greg is no exception.

British Royal Air Force
18th RAF Fighter Wing
Cheltenham RAF Fighter Base
Nottingham, Great Britain

10 August 1940
2nd Lt Greg Levenson
c/o Moody AFB
Valdosta, GA USA

Lt Levenson:

Your name has been highly recommended for recruitment by Lt Andy Mamedoff, a member of the American Eagle Squadron, with whom you trained at Moody a while back. As I am sure you are aware the Eagle Squadron is helping us Brits out as best they can but we are in a helluva scrape. Intelligence sources have pegged the number of German fighters at about 2,800 compared to our 600 Spitfires and Hurricanes. While we have certain advantages such as a new early-warning radar system and a well-coordinated air defense we are still up against it and need the assistance of a pilot of your caliber.

The consequences of losing what may prove to be one of the most crucial battles in history are clear. If we lose air superiority and Hitler is able to launch an invasion, it will be that much harder to strike at the heart of Germany and establish a base for the inevitable invasion of occupied Europe.

I will not deceive you by saying that what you will face will be anything but trying. There is no real pilot rotation, and it is not uncommon for most of us to fly days on end without respite. We have been forced to use enlisted pilots, and while they give it a go, they are certainly not the quality of an experienced pilot like yourself.

The Jerries come at us daily in overwhelming waves but somehow we are holding our own with the help of a considerable number of non-British pilots like Mamedoff. Hence this letter. He raved about your exceptional air-to-air combat skills, tenacity, determination, and grit. Also, he said you are a fine chap who can mix quite nicely with the hodgepodge of British and multi-national fighter pilots making up our force.

There is one more consideration you should know before making a decision, i.e., the Jewish factor. From your name I gathered that like Mamedoff you are Jewish and therefore you must feel for what is going on in Europe under the Nazis. What may surprise you is that I as well am a Jew, much to the surprise (and chagrin?) of my mates. In fact I recently listed my name with the RAF Jewish Chaplaincy in the event of my death.

I was nothing more than a nominal Jew until the war started but since then I have found myself to be more identified as such. I'm sorry that it took the war to bring this about, but as you Yanks say, "Better late than never."

Interestingly enough, there are about 30 Jewish pilots (from 6 different countries) flying with us. They have accounted for themselves quite well. One of them recently said that knowing that his people are being slaughtered on the ground gives him great satisfaction to destroy the enemy in the air. I am also convinced that this awareness gives us a bit of an edge. Anyway, I mention this not to unduly pressure you (too much) but I thought you ought to have a complete picture before you decide.

Time is of the essence so we would appreciate a hasty response. In the meantime keep us in your thoughts and wish us Godspeed.

Thank you for your time and attention.

Many regards,

Flt Lt Robert S. Tuck

18th RAF Fighter Wing

Cheltenham RAF Fighter Base

Nottingham, Great Britain

P.S. One of our recent losses was a fine young chap named Sgt Stephen A. Levenson. Any relation?

CHAPTER 14

Determined at Birth

"Character is not determined at birth. With free will we ourselves decide what we become."

—Jewish meditation, for consideration prior to holy days

IN 2005, GREG WAS MARRIED IN AUSTIN, TEXAS, where he had attended college. Several hundred people were present. Among them were two combat veterans featured in this book. One was the aforementioned Maj. Gen. James Breedlove USAF (Ret.) and the other Sgt. Bernie Barasch. Both were positive male role models who served their country with distinction in Vietnam and World War II, respectively.

That night I got it in my head that the two had to meet. After all, there was no way that the only awardees of the Distinguished Flying Cross in the room shouldn't get to know each other. So I got up from the dinner before finishing, interrupted Bernie, and walked him to the other side of the ballroom to find Jim. Bernie was delighted. He lit up when he met the general. Jim could not have been more gracious. Their mutual appreciation for what they had in common was clear—two combat veterans who served their country with distinction. It was a very nice moment.

Greg received his wings on April 23, 2006. It was shortly thereafter he progressed to the rigorous four-month-long Introduction to Fighter Fundamentals (IFF) training program at Moody AFB in Valdosta, Georgia. Greg's problems that summer were complicated by my being diagnosed with a potentially lethal form of cancer on June 6, 2006. The seriousness of the diagnosis was reflected in the strict instructions I received a few weeks later at MD Anderson Cancer Center in Houston. I was pointedly told not to take any long vacations before I started chemotherapy.

On June 23, 2006, I began receiving a very powerful combination of four cancer-killing drugs, after which I faced a complicated surgery with a long recovery. When I expressed fears about the procedure, the oncologist in Houston advised me to just worry about one thing at a time. He told us that the chemotherapy could kill me as easily as the cancer could. Every other week for eight weeks I was injected with a noxious cocktail, and I have never been sicker.

At the conclusion of the chemotherapy, the aforementioned Gen. Breedlove, one of Greg's most significant inspirations, made an unexpected but indelible impact. He generously opened his home in Horseshoe Bay, Texas, only an hour from MD Anderson, to use the weekend before I was to have surgery.

Just prior to the operation that was to save my life, he firmly informed me that I had spent my career taking care of others, and now it was my turn to let them take care of me. He added that he *expected* me to follow my doctors' instructions to a T. After I hung up the phone, it hit me that I had just been given a direct order from a two-star general! I had no choice but to survive.

I was tested to the extreme during this period of my life, as was my family—including Greg, whom I did not want distracted in any way during this critical phase of training. One verity is that a fighter pilot must possess two essential qualities: situational awareness and the ability to multitask. To those I would add a third: compartmentalization, a trait that served Greg well during the half-year or so of my illness and recovery. All of this time coincided with some phase of Greg's flight training and combat experience.

Greg consistently found a way to come through for me. He showed up in Lubbock during the worst parts of the chemotherapy, again in Houston following the twelve-hour surgery, and yet again during my hospital stay. I found Greg to be quietly supportive and receptive to the end-of-life conversations I felt obligated to have with him.

At this time I realized that the tables had been ironically turned. The teacher had become the student. I needed inspiration to keep going, and fortunately—because of my recent research—it was a short stretch to apply to myself the historical examples I offered to Greg. They seemed to help me, just as I know that they helped Greg.

Until I became deathly ill in 2006, prayer for me was mostly perfunctory. I recited the requisite Jewish ritual and holiday prayers without much thought. As a result, I was virtually blind to the power of prayer and how it would play an unexpected part in my life.

I only remember directly asking God to answer my prayers on three occasions. My first memory of this type of intercessory prayer was a most lighthearted one, when I was sixteen years old. I was on a summer baseball team comprising mostly high school players I was trying to impress in my quest to make the Nottingham varsity. At the time, nothing seemed more important.

I started on the bench as usual, when something remarkable occurred. Our pitcher, Dave Phillips, was systematically mowing down the opposition. In fact, he was pitching a perfect game.

Normally, I couldn't wait to get into a game, but this game was different. I prayed that I would be overlooked. I didn't want to be the one to spoil Dave's gem. When I was put in during a defensive change, I remember praying, "Please God, don't let them hit the ball to me."

This prayer wasn't answered. Two balls came my way, and I made both plays. The perfect game was intact.

The second incident occurred on the day the space shuttle *Challenger* blew up. I knew that I would be asked to do the school intervention where Christa McAuliffe taught because of a previous intervention I did involving a school shooting, but I prayed that the phone wouldn't ring. I distinctly remember feeling the pressure and watching the push button light up. I knew immediately I was being beckoned. I was later told by the principal that I did what was needed.

The last time I talked with God was during my recovery. Life-threatening chemotherapy and major reconstructive surgery were behind me. I had no body fat, looked like walking death, and was weak as a kitten. I was home by then and trying to do physical therapy in order to regain my stamina.

Suddenly I reached the limits of whatever strength I had left. I collapsed onto a tile floor, and then and there I told God that I was more than okay with his taking me.

Nothing happened, so I picked myself up and weakly kept going. Later I realized that I had more life to live and people to help. I evolved into a better therapist. I am grateful that God wasn't ready for me.

An ancient Jewish adage goes: "A person who arises from prayer a better person has their prayer answered." I'd like to think that for me this is exactly what happened.

Shortly after I was diagnosed and started chemotherapy, a relative of my mother-in-law shared my predicament with her small Baptist church in Silverton, Texas. (My wife had converted from Baptist to Judaism as a teenager.) Their immediate response was for several of the congregants to write me notes of faith, hope, and encouragement every Wednesday. At first I was surprised to receive the prayers but soon I began to look forward to reading them. The notes were brief, concise, and powerful.

I am still not one who expects God to answer my prayers directly. This expectation opens up too many unanswerable questions, such as why some people's prayers are answered and others are not. When this question is posed, I prefer to think that the answer lies in one's response to the challenge faced.

Gradually, I became overwhelmed—in a good way—by the good-will expressed by these people of faith entirely unknown to me who prayed on my behalf. I began feeling obligated to them and pushed myself even harder during my long recovery. It is one thing to be aware of my family and close friends supporting me. But to know that my support team was greatly expanded by the Southern Baptists in Silverton (as well as a local Lubbock Baptist church, which also included me in their prayers) strengthened my resolve and reinforced my faith in God.

The notes continued for about two months during the course of my recovery. I missed them when they stopped. At that time I appreciated the power of prayer and a handwritten letter.

Letter writing is intensely personal. Someone has to take the time and effort to gather a pen, paper, envelope, stamp, and an address, and then sit down and thoughtfully convey what needs to be said. In today's world of electronic communication, handwritten letters are becoming obsolete as social media with all its grammatical shortcuts and misspellings dominate interpersonal communications.

While writing this book I was pleased to learn that I was not the only person who sent Greg letters regularly. His grandmother Opal Keith, the same person who helped arrange the Silverton Baptists' notes, wrote to him during his F-16 training at Luke AFB in Phoenix, Arizona.

Opal's letters were mostly about her upbringing and Greg's roots on his mother's side of the family. In her correspondence, Opal described her life growing up in a farm family in Tulia, Texas. At that time Opal and I never discussed our motivations for our letter writing, but in retrospect we were very much on the same page. Both of us were strengthening Greg's identity by reinforcing his spiritual and familial foundations, but from different perspectives. At Luke our purposes merged into one and Greg was that much better for it.

When I was sick, I only remember weeping once. Prior to the major reconstructive surgery I was to have at MD Anderson in 2006, I had about three or four days of tests and surgical preparation. Of all my friends and family there was one person I *needed* to see: my former employer in Houston eighteen years earlier, Bob Weinberger.

Bob and I had maintained only occasional contact in all that time, but he was still first on my list. To say that we had a contentious working relationship would be a gross understatement. Our conflicts were about professional matters and never personal, but they were nevertheless volatile and intense.

We worked on a locked unit full of the most disturbed adolescents from the greater Houston area. The unit was a veritable pressure cooker. Some of the kids had been there for months and were only permitted limited contact with their families and the outside world. I worked with them individually, with their families, and in groups.

Bob was an energetic, creative, and at times unconventional therapist. The extreme disorders of the kids and the therapeutic environment in which they were confined brought out the best and worst in Bob. Our clashes were usually about clinical tactics and the role writ large of a therapist on a locked unit.

At this time in my career, my work clearly defined me. Being sick caused me to reflect on it and all those who helped me develop my skills. Bob stood head and shoulders above all of them. So, in spite of our conflicts, I respected him for how under his supervision most of the deeply troubled teens got better and were able to live normal lives.

Bob responded immediately to my request, and he came to see me in the hospital, matzah ball soup in hand. There we reminisced about our time together, and he told me what I most needed to hear. He affirmed my value as a mental health provider by saying, "you are the most effective therapist working with adolescents that I have ever seen." Coming from Bob, this meant everything, especially at this critical time, and I was brought to tears.

The life-and-death predicament I found myself in also guided me to a little-known Jewish tradition. Prior to one's death a Jew has the option of writing what is known as an "ethical will." Essentially, it is a statement to be read at the funeral, which speaks to how the decedent wishes to be remembered. It also states how Judaism provided inspiration for the decedent and how it can inspire others.

Early in my career as an emergency services psychologist, I was thrust into several potentially life-threatening situations, so I was forced to think that an ethical will would be in order. In 1986 I wrote one and put it away for posterity, never really thinking about it ever being read.

Twenty years later with my life on the line I pulled out the ethical will. While it held up over time and didn't require revisions, the question became who would read it. The key was to find someone who knew me but who was not so close that they might have difficulty reading something so deeply personal.

When Greg decided to become a pilot, I had the good fortune to know many of the men who trained him and with whom he would serve. One of them, Lt. Col. Ryan McGuire, was instrumental in encouraging Greg to believe in himself and make his dream a reality.

Over the years, I had come to know Ryan fairly well, and it became obvious that he was the perfect choice for my unusual request. I asked him to do this favor for me, and he unhesitatingly consented. I sent him the will; he read it once and then put it in his safe deposit box, where it is today.

An Air Force saying that is used to indicate a pilot's success on a bombing mission is "On time and on target." My family learned during surgery that the surgeons were successful and able to cut away enough cancerous tissue to achieve clear margins and help reduce the spread of the disease. The chemo had worked! It was exactly what the medical team was hoping for when they started the surgery. While in postoperative recovery I received an overnight delivery package from Greg with a model F-16 inside. Enclosed with the model was a note that simply read, "On time, on target!"

In the summer of 2007 Greg officially became a combat-mission-qualified fighter pilot with the New Mexico Air National Guard

150th Fighter Squadron. By a fluke of fate, in October 2007 he was selected to join his squadron when it was deployed to Balad AFB, Iraq. It usually takes longer—if it happens at all—for a trained fighter pilot to see action, but he got the opportunity to do very early in his career what he was trained to do. We were now officially a Blue Star family.[20]

In the forty-five days or so that Greg was in a combat theater, he flew nineteen sorties and was called upon to engage the enemy on four occasions. He was on time and on target, but I will let his commendations speak for his success. Greg went to war with a J (Jewish) dog tag in spite of the inherent risks.

An interesting side note regarding these missions reveals much about Greg's character. Each time he flew in combat he took with him a small American flag. At the completion of each mission, he sent one to a loved one whom he felt provided support to him above and beyond what would normally be expected.

The flags were personalized and encased in a framed plaque. One was sent to my niece Jill Potash and reads, "This flag was flown over liberated Iraq aboard an F-16C Falcon from the 150th Fighter Wing, the most lethal platform in theater. This flag has been supersonic over the skies of Iraq so that the Iraqi people could hear the sound of freedom."

I never doubted that Greg would be prepared and capable when called upon to do his job, but I was not prepared to learn of his other activities in the combat theater. Greg's second commendation cites his work in the Balad AFB Theater Hospital, where he met the incoming helicopters, helped carry litters into the hospital, and stayed with the injured—Americans and Iraqis alike—while they were being triaged for treatment.

What I found ironic about his choice of how to use his off time was that I could never get him to go on hospital rounds with me to see the

---

20 With the role of Blue Star parents suddenly thrust upon us, my wife, Carol, and I had to make some major adjustments of our own. For example, late one evening, the doorbell unexpectedly rang, and both of us instantly experienced that awful feeling in the pit of our stomachs. We reluctantly went to the door fearing the presence of two Air Force bereavement officers, only to find a lost pizza delivery man!

inpatient aspect of my practice. (I'd obtain permission from the patient and family before doing so.) I am called upon to evaluate and treat trauma patients as well as the chronically ill for emotional issues such as PTSD, depression, anxiety, and adjustment problems. In the twenty years I had done this as part of my practice he never accompanied me, and I considered the issue closed. He clearly wanted no part of that aspect of my work, and I could hardly blame him.

In Iraq, his perspective changed. He volunteered when he was off duty to do what he could do for the many casualties he witnessed. Greg's air medal is very special and confirms his place as a highly proficient fighter pilot, but I have to admit that his Air Force Achievement Medal means more to me. His first-grade ribbon for kindness had evolved.

A primary treatment intervention for trauma victims and their families is to reframe the event by making something positive derive from the trauma. By doing so, memories of the trauma are transformed from something life-threatening (or -ending) to ones that are life-affirming. An example of this was Greg's decision to establish a scholarship at the high school of a fallen soldier he knew briefly. This act proved to aid in the healing of the decedent's parents, and they greatly appreciated the gesture. Greg did this entirely on his own without my consultation.

And we now have a running joke about whether he is ready to go with me on rounds. His answer is always a quick "Never."

During the time between completion of the last draft of this manuscript and its going into production for printing, I have maintained a fervent interest in the book's subject matter. While my research in no way has been systematic, further readings have revealed some incredible stories of Jewish military participation that until recently have been overlooked.

One involves young immigrant German Jewish soldiers who returned to Europe and made a major contribution to the war effort.

As reported in Bruce Henderson's *Sons and Soldiers*, a large group of Jewish children under the age of sixteen were allowed to leave Europe and go to America in the 1930s. When the war started a few years later these same (male) children were now of age to serve. By then, Nazi atrocities were well known, and these young men were ready to return to Europe with a vengeance.

One of the least understood aspects of the Second World War was the urgency that operations demanded. Time meant lives, and the United States was all about minimizing casualties. This issue was never more apparent than during preparations for the Normandy invasion.

The Army at that time realized that vital German-speaking interpreters would be necessary after the invasion for intelligence purposes, but such people were in short supply. It was only logical that there would be significant numbers of bilingual soldiers among the aforementioned group of relatively recent immigrant inductees. Over eighteen hundred were identified from their enlistment records, and they were quickly put into their specialized service.

D-Day was fast approaching, so these men were selected out and assigned to various combat units, including airborne infantry, which was the tip of the spear. The only problem was the little time available to prepare these men for battle. As a result they had only the bare minimum of combat and parachute training. Henderson tells an amusing anecdote about how some of the interpreters learned to parachute out of an airplane by jumping off wooden crates in a hangar just days before the invasion! These brave, now fully American soldiers went in anyway and served their country with distinction. At least fifty were killed in action.

A second example relates to who was most likely the last combat casualty of World War II, a nineteen-year-old Jewish fighter pilot from Brooklyn, New York, by the name of Lt. Philip Schlamberg. His story is described in Don Brown and Jerry Yellin's excellent book, *The Last Fighter Pilot*. In it, Capt. Yellin, Schlamberg's flight leader on the last combat mission of the war on August 14, 1945, tells of a premonition Schlamberg had on that fateful day.

Lt. Schlamberg told Yellin that he felt he wouldn't return with the rest of the squadron. Yellin took him seriously, spoke to the squadron commander on his behalf, and Schlamberg was given the option of remaining behind. With a sense of dread, he bluntly refused. He had come this far with his men, and he was determined to complete the mission, especially since it was so close to the end of the war. The second atomic bomb had been dropped on Nagasaki five days earlier, and the pilots were anxiously awaiting the code word "Ohio" to signify a Japanese surrender.

After strafing an airfield near Tokyo, Yellin's squadron reassembled for the return trip to Iwo Jima. Only Schlamberg failed to appear. His plane and remains were never found. Very shortly thereafter, the Japanese surrendered, making Schlamberg the last known serviceman killed in action. His exemplary service earned him an Air Medal with two oak leaf clusters and a Purple Heart.

There were most certainly Jewish casualties when the Nazis invaded Poland on September 1, 1939, the first day of World War II. This assumption is based on the fact that over thirty thousand Polish Jews died defending Poland during the course of the war. While the first Polish combat death may not have been Jewish, the point of this story is yet again supported. The war was bookended by Jewish military participation, not to mention all these Jews who honorably and courageously served in between. There was no "Jewish Quartermaster Corps," that mythical group of combat-avoidant Jews, on any front at any time.

CHAPTER 15

To Love Someone

"To love someone is not just a strong feeling—it is a decision, it is a judgment, it is a promise."

—Erich Fromm, *The Art of Loving* (2013)

A Word from the Pilot

THE FOUNDING FATHERS OFTEN REFERRED TO "providence," and I've had a lot of it in my life. I was born in the United States, a gift in itself, at a time of relative peace and prosperity. I have parents who love me and have had the ability to provide more than I deserve but who were also willing to encourage my dreams and soften my failures. Having both men and women whom I admired in my own family who served in the military is most likely what spawned my early interest in the subject. I grew up in an Air Force town, home to Reese Air Force Base, which included regular field trips to that base and regular contact with young aviators around town. There may have been brief moments when I dreamed of becoming a firefighter or a doctor, but mostly my memory is filled with a deep passion for aviation and a respect for those who took to the air in support of the nation.

Greg Levenson and fighter.

It didn't feel particularly lucky that my parents divorced when I was young. Being a bit overweight and interested in history, of all things, already made me feel as though I stood apart from my peers. The loss of what I had considered a normal home life stung. But providence would play a regular role in my life and this time intertwine Norman Shulman's life with my own. It was the first night of a spring break cruise aboard the SS *Norway* (formerly the SS *France* and a historic vessel in its own right) that my mother, grandmother, and I discovered that our assigned mealtime seats for the week would be at a table with Norm. In the thirty-five years since, Norm has regularly served as confidant, cheerleader, guide, educator, therapist, mediator, sounding board, and friend—all of the characteristics of a parent extraordinaire! In our very small Jewish community, Norm also served as part-time rabbi to many and prepared me for my Bar Mitzvah while being a full-time example of living a Jewish life and having a Jewish identity.

Ultimately, I delayed my entry into the Air Force until the relatively late age of twenty-six. I had a stereotypical college experience and, given the end of the Cold War in the 1990s, I thought I'd I missed my chance to participate in history through military service. In the wake of September 11, 2001, however, our nation clearly would need people passionate about its future. I felt it was time for me to set aside, if only for the time being, a more traditional career in exchange for service to the nation. That unfortunately struck a large number of my family and friends as odd, if not something worse. I learned to more quickly retort that I wanted to share something in common with Washington, Grant, and Hap Arnold. The final example of patriotism did the trick to turn the conversation back to a polite history lesson around the father of the Air Force. I kept to myself what would have been more regrettable retorts.

My application to become an Air Force pilot felt a lot like trying to get into an Ivy League school. After a series of tests, essentially academic and hand–eye coordination, I was assigned a Pilot Candidate Selection Method score high enough to at least qualify for flight training. I opted for a path that would place me with an Air National Guard Wing after active-duty training. This would, I hoped, allow me to return to my banking career in short order and at the same time continue a military career on a part-time basis. The process humbled me (the training would later finish that job), and I came to see that I couldn't approach this application in same manner as I would have for a bank career; the life-and-death stakes of those who held the job require a different set of personality characteristics. After the second rejection to become a pilot, I sat in a lawn chair on the grass, beer in hand, and told Norm I had had enough rejection. It was time to move on with the banking career. He listened and agreed that I had a path already carved, but he added that only the third strike really causes an out. He asked if I could move forward with a banking career and at the same time take one more swing at the application. It was certainly providential to have him push me, because that third application was my home run.

All of a sudden, the stars seemed to be lining up for me. Every obstacle fell aside, even when the odds were stacked against me. As an example, I failed a hearing test, likely the result of hunting without hearing protection as a kid, and somehow got a waiver that I was told was impossible. Then, before my enlistment, my training dates were set more than a year into the future, and just as I questioned the path, a new training date opened weeks away and I was off to Officer Candidate School. In a moment of real emotion, my grandmother, one of the very first women to serve in the Navy as a WAVE, pinned on my second lieutenant's gold bar, making me an officer in the United States Air Force. Norm traveled with her (my mother was recovering from major knee surgery) and sat smiling in the stands as I marched past on parade at my graduation. Norm, like no one else in my life, had been there to commiserate over the failed applications, encourage just one more try, and celebrate the moment I became an officer in the USAF.

Tradition has it that after receiving their first-ever salute from an enlisted airman, a newly commissioned officer gives that airman a real pre-1965 silver dollar. At that moment, most officers fully realize they are wearing the rank and beginning a path of great responsibility. Roughly three weeks after giving away my silver dollar, I checked in at Vance Air Force Base, where I was quickly reminded that, in fact, I wasn't so special or fantastic. On an Air Force base that trains pilots, nonpilot officers have lesser status than pilot officers. What counted here was that gleaming pair of wings to be hard earned and placed on my chest. Whatever hardships I thought I had overcome in high school athletics or college scholastics were trivial to the work that the next year of pilot training would entail. It only took a week or two before I had been beaten down mentally if not physically, feeling awful about my abilities and chances at success. Then a letter arrived.

Norm started with one letter and continued week after week through the yearlong course. The training was demoralizing at times and always exhausting. I called home to Norm, telling him about the challenges at hand, and instead of trying to rally my spirit with a few words he went to work to find the history he knew would speak to my soul. I found inspiration in the accounts that Norm had specially selected to fit the challenging year of Undergraduate Pilot Training. From the Maccabees through the American Revolution, World War I and on to Iraq, the letters offered a chronicle of heroism and triumph despite challenge. The stories were primarily of other Jews at their best in combat, and the letters provided me with the answer to questions from friends and family such as, "Why would a nice Jewish boy like you join the military?" or from the few, mostly innocently ignorant, folks who learned of my faith and said, "I didn't know Jews were in the military." When I finished each week's letter, it was a little easier to push ahead and go back for more.

At the end of the year, to honor his support and recognize the deep bond we had built, I gave Norm half of my first pair of wings in keeping with Air Force tradition. To preserve good luck a pilot's first pair of wings is broken in two, with a best friend keeping half and the pilot keeping the other half. I was clearly lucky to have been in a position to earn those wings, and providence had given me Norm to be among those who held me up when I felt least able.

When driving across the country to Moody Air Force Base and my next level of training, I learned that Norm had been diagnosed with a rare and difficult-to-treat cancer. Checking in to Introduction to Fighter Fundamentals (IFF), I was more nervous than excited. The course was known to be difficult with a high washout rate, and the humid South Georgia summer added to my perspiration. I did my best to draw on the letters' inspiration, but it was hard, knowing that the storyteller himself was lying in a hospital bed near death.

I was so focused on finishing the IFF course that I never bothered to tell any of my supervisors that I was distracted, my mind often drifting to Houston and the MD Anderson Cancer Center. It was an important life lesson. By the time I did finally reach out for help, I was one formal review with the commander away from washing out. But the value of friendships and great leadership came through when a senior officer from the New Mexico Air National Guard, my future unit, flew out to coach me through that conversation with the "boss."

It's what's known in the Air Force as a "floor save"—those times when the aircraft is just about to crash but through extreme effort, application of all the pilot's skills, and a little luck the aircraft is saved from hitting the floor (ground). It was the comeback story of my life, and I couldn't have been happier to get in my car and drive away with a diploma in hand. I had even graduated alone several days after my class because the commander had been generous enough to give me a week to gather my thoughts and perform at the level required to complete the course. Two days later I was in Arizona to begin my F-16 training.

Long before I ever piloted the single-engine, single-pilot fighter that could drop bombs and shoot a gun, the F-16 Fighting Falcon had quickened my pulse. Known to its pilots as the Viper, the F-16 has long been a mainstay of the Air Force, capable of a wide array of missions. Its radical maneuverability led the USAF Thunderbirds demonstration team to select it for their performances, where it's served since 1983. In Arizona I had my first experience with the Viper's beautiful lines and heart-stopping performance. Stepping out of my two-door sports car at Luke Air Force Base felt cinematic. The roar of a full afterburner takeoff echoed against the hangars while I looked up to behold a flawless two-ship formation pattern. The radiating joy of being there took away all my angst about my performance in the previous months. I was here to earn my place as a fighter pilot and better yet pilot the very fighter that I had dreamed of since childhood. My time at Luke was almost always one of happiness and acceptance into the fighter-pilot community and the Air Force family as a whole. Everything I had done before was necessary to get here, but during F-16 training I wanted simply to learn all I could about that fabulous machine and how to employ it in combat. I was never again threatened with washing out but admit that I rarely threatened to be the top performer in the class either.

I firmly believe that the men and women of the Air Force don't get enough credit for who they are and what they represent. The melting

Greg (standing in foreground) with fellow pilots selected to go to Iraq. Kirtland Air Force Base, 2007.

pot of America has long burned hot in the Air Force. Whether it's a discussion around race, religion, gender, education, socioeconomic background, or even citizenship, one can rest assured that the Air Force is stirring the pot and is better for it—becoming more diversified and more accepting of minorities in general. The examples date back to the earliest days of the Army Air Corps, but recent examples also abound. In August 2020 Charles Q. Brown, whom I have not met but know to be one of the finest fighter pilots to ever exist and one of the best of Americans, took command of the Air Force as the first African American chief of staff of any branch of service. He assumed office from David Goldfein, who gave the address at my graduation, the second Jewish American to hold the chief of staff position. Likewise, in 2020 JoAnne Bass rose to be the chief master sergeant of the Air Force and thereby became the first female to lead the enlisted force of any branch of the military and first person of Asian American descent to hold the position in the Air Force. These men and women are the latest examples of a force full of individuals who are impressive not because of the roles they hold but rather because of the people they are. The community is as full of scientists and engineers as it is of mechanics who will work through the night on complex machines and personalists who love and care for the airmen like they are family. I love the Air Force and always will because of those with whom I was honored to share the experience.

As full mugs of beer clanked together in celebration of St. Patrick's Day and my graduation from F-16 school, Norm was finally healthy enough again to share one (I might have had more than just one). It was off to school one last time before I joined the combat side of the Air Force, referred to as the CAF. This time it was the training program at Fairchild Air Force Base known as Survival, Evasion, Resistance, and Escape (SERE). It's a school that no one really looks forward to and yet everyone leaves feeling stronger from having experienced.

After years of dreaming, I was finally part of a bona fide fighter squadron, the 150th Fighter Wing of the New Mexico Air National Guard, often referred to as the Tacos. The wing was preparing for deployment to Iraq in support of Operation Iraqi Freedom, and I wanted nothing more than to be part of the deployment. As the departure date rapidly approached, I cajoled my commanders daily to let me complete all the necessary tasks to qualify. When the tasking was drawn up, I was listed as the first alternate. I'm confident that the same commander who had come down to Georgia to coach me through my plea to stay in IFF had worked behind the scenes to at least get me on the list as an alternate. I owe him as much as anyone when it comes to my Air Force career. Most people felt it was unlikely for the alternate to make the trip. Luck reached up and pulled me into the lineup just two weeks before departure. Unfortunately for one of my fellow pilots, a water main had broken in front of his house, creating a sinkhole that swallowed all they owned. Thankfully no one was harmed, but he felt he had to stay behind and help his family get through the displacement. Even more unexpected was that he was one of twelve pilots slated to fly an aircraft from New Mexico to Iraq.

Given the late change it was decided that I would move entirely into his boots and fly a jet halfway around the world despite the fact that I was the least experienced pilot in our deployment.

The early-morning takeoff was the beginning of the most heart-pounding, tear-jerking, ear-to-ear smiling, and accomplished period in my life. The first leg of the crossing was set to depart Kirtland Air Force Base in New Mexico in the middle of the night with a dedicated tanker for air refueling across the continent. We would travel using the call sign "Mazda" rather than our normal "Taco" handle and reach the East Coast as the sun rose, where we'd meet up with a second tanker to take us across the Atlantic to Spain. The vast expanses of the US West gave way to the spiderwebs of interconnected lights lining highways and cities of the Midwest.

Somewhere around Chicago we got word that the tanker scheduled to meet us off the coast of Massachusetts had a mechanical issue and wouldn't be there. It was a lesson in planning and preparing backups I never forgot. The F-16 is akin to an Indy race car in that once you're inside, it's a comfortable reclining seat with everything you need to fly and employ the aircraft right at your fingertips. The pilot never needs to lean over to reach a switch or bend down to pick something up from the floor. For the most part you can't lean or bend anywhere because there is nowhere to go inside the famous glass bubble canopy, and prior to our takeoff I had carefully organized my charts and maps for all that I thought I would need to get from New Mexico to our scheduled stop in the south of Spain. But in the dark of night, we were discovering that all of the Air Force bases that I had considered as possible emergency landing sites were not open for us to come through without a real emergency, and technically all our jets were working just fine.

The airport we ended up at was in Bangor, Maine, and home to the tanker that had brought us from New Mexico. It was scheduled to land there, and the crews that would be helping to secure the four-engine gas station in the sky would be able to help us at this early hour. As I tried to dig out the charts for a nighttime approach to an unfamiliar airfield, I got word that light rain and low clouds would greet us in Bangor. Suddenly my cockpit seemed to fill with the humidity of my own perspiration as I leafed through hundreds of pages of charts and maps that had been neatly packed together like a novel. I finally got the approach plates for Bangor and stuffed dozens of now unneeded items between my ejection seat and the side panels of the cockpit as our formation began to descend through the clouds. The planning had been perfect, and indeed we reached the East Coast just as the sun rose. As the first guys were landing in Bangor, the rays peeked over the horizon with a pale pink glow, all of the little droplets of water from the clouds and drizzle catching the peach shade of the morning. I finally related to those old documentaries I'd watched where a pilot would say something like, "I was in the soup."

My smile faded quickly as the first jet landed and radioed a report to the rest of us behind him. The visibility was deteriorating by the minute, and I would be the last to land. I knew it was critical that we all stay together and that we get these jets to the theater of operation where they were scheduled to be put into combat within hours of their arrival. Coached by the far more experienced aviators landing in front of me, I was told to expect to see the "rabbit," the three thousand or more feet of sequenced strobes aligned with the runway centerline just before the runway begins. I knew that was their way of saying the visibility was below what we needed but they trusted I could do it and it needed to be done. I never saw the rabbit. I flew the plane using the instruments of the heads-up display and saw the two runway-end identifier lights zoom past at two hundred miles per hour as my jet crossed the threshold and touched down gently about one second later.

This was the confidence boost that I needed as I headed off to combat only a few months from graduating from F-16 school. I had great training and could fly this airplane in all circumstances to do what was needed. I'm sure I was taller when I got out of the jet, perhaps looking a little less cool with my flight suit drenched in my own sweat, but certainly feeling like King Kong. The rest of the trip to Iraq was no less an adventure. Seeing the coast of Europe, I couldn't help but think of Lindbergh and the first time he saw it. We passed right over the Strait of Gibraltar before landing in Spain, and I took in the sight of two continents that looked just a short swim apart. The next day we again took flight in the darkness of night to be greeted by foul weather over the Mediterranean, making midair refueling sketchy. The clouds cleared by the time the turquoise-blue waters gave way to the perfectly tan coastline of Egypt. Passing over the Nile River Valley I craned my neck, without success, to find the Great Pyramids. Over the wind-blown mountains of sand in Saudi Arabia we gassed up one last time and said good-bye to the tanker as they took a right turn toward Qatar, and we turned left for Iraq. The flight lead gave a quick pep talk, let the radio go silent for just a breath, and made the most memorable radio call of my life, "Mazda Flight, fence in!"

"Fence in" is the instruction to aircraft that they are crossing the imaginary fence separating peace from combat. The message is to take threats seriously, to arm weapons, and to keep your head on a swivel looking for anything that might be after you. My hand moved quickly to arm the defensive ordnance we were carrying, and I went a full minute before realizing it was all right if I continued to draw breath.

I felt lost in another world as we arrived at Balad Air Force Base. In midst of the Sunni Triangle, the base is forty miles northwest of Baghdad and had been one of Saddam's largest before it was taken over by Coalition forces in 2003. Four years later it had been transformed into a sprawling US-run facility with all makes of aircraft and vehicles rumbling like ceaseless waves crashing ashore, no matter the day or time. It was during the so-called surge of 2007, and an influx of US servicepeople swelled the ranks of US forces across the country, now using tactics that were aimed at more aggressively stamping out the insurgency. The air was almost always acrid, with black smoke rising from sources around the base or from the fire pit burning the trash.

Streets had been paved connecting miles of buildings to hold aircraft and dining facilities, the theater hospital, and thousands upon thousands of single-wide trailers used for housing.

There was almost no color. It was like living in a brown and gray movie scene filmed on another planet. Uniforms were versions of the same color as the sand on the ground, the sky rarely turned blue, and all the buildings blended together in a mauve tone. This pale world intensified the few colors that did exist—in the blast shields painted with patches of units that had spent time on base and the ubiquitous American flag that flew proudly almost everywhere.

It didn't take long for me to go from feeling lost in this world to feeling the world was lost to me. Everything in a combat environment is straightforward. The men and women around me were focused on their job just as I was, and ultimately we held the same mission. For the several months I was in Balad, I dressed the same every day. Almost without exception I ate at the same location for every meal, and so did just about everyone I knew. Money had no meaning, nor did any sense of envy for, or pride in, material things. Life was fairly simple. Go to work, give it your all, make a difference, don't do anything stupid, exercise and stay hydrated in the desert, and sleep when you need it. To relax I played chess with friends or got a cup of coffee; there was no alcohol available—or much of anything beyond coffee and adrenaline.

If I had free time I volunteered at the hospital. It's hard for people who haven't had a similar experience to fully understand, but I was happy there. Almost immediately I began writing letters home. Mostly they were mass emails as my time available with a computer was limited, and I was never sure how my words might sound to ears not seeing and feeling the same things as I did every day. I often thought of Norm's weekly letters and understood that they were intended to pull me through the trying days of training, but now it was my turn. I felt it was my obligation, in fact, to add to the history already written. It was my turn to stand on their shoulders and assure all those men and women to whom Norm had introduced me would be proud to have me join them.

My squadron had a combat tradition dating to the Korean War of the least experienced flight lead being paired with the least experienced wingman for the wingman's first combat sortie. It is the ultimate chest-pounding display of confidence in the airmanship of both pilots and has never failed to be a complete success. Now there I was, a freshly minted F-16 pilot who had graduated from the F-16 schoolhouse just a few months earlier, heading out with a flight lead, call sign "Danny," who had been upgraded to flight lead just a few weeks earlier. I'm certain we both quietly recited Alan Shepard's famous prayer: "Dear Lord, please don't let me fuck this up."

Just as we checked in with the ground forces we were set to support, Danny's jet had an alternator failure. It wasn't a serious emergency, but it was time for him to go back to base and get a working jet. We both anticipated that I would be headed back with him, but on the return to base the folks at Central Command made it clear that we had one working jet and there was no reason to bring that jet back on the ground and risk a mishap during landing. I would be left airborne, alone, supporting ground forces within ten miles of the base. It would take Danny roughly an hour to land, get a replacement, and get back to me. I offered up in my cockpit through gritted teeth a full-throated recitation of Alan Shepard's prayer.

I watched Danny land safely and turned my radio over to the channel of the local ground forces. Balad was affectionately known as "Mortaritaville" because of the sometimes-hourly indiscriminate rocket and mortar attacks against it. Insurgents would get close enough to the base to launch a few and then drive away as fast as they could. F-16s returning to base with extra gas, or in my case waiting on a flight lead to get back in the air, would circle the base searching out suspicious vehicles or groups of people. After about fifteen minutes I realized I needed to find an airborne tanker and get gas sometime soon. I again pulled out all my charts, this time well organized to find anything I could possibly need, and let the joint terminal air controller who was working with the ground troops know I would be headed off for fuel. I sighed with relief that nothing had been fired at the base while I was overhead and turned west to where my maps indicated a tanker would be positioned. Then it hit me like ice water being poured over my head. I had never, in peacetime or combat, gone to a tanker alone. Sure, a week ago I took gas roughly twenty times between New Mexico and Iraq, but that was more than all the experiences I had before combined—and then I was simply following a flight lead to the designated spot and listening to him work the radios and choose when and how to line up with a fifty-year-old airplane carrying two hundred thousand pounds of fuel.

Nothing can substitute for good training. I'm not sure how I did it except through rote memory, even though in very real ways it was the first time. I'm sure my voice gave away my lack of confidence, but I found the tanker track and saw the giant as it turned in the sky as I made my radio call announcing my approach. I made a nearly perfect lead turn to place my F-16 just where I had wanted to be behind the left wing, a few hundred yards back. The refueling was textbook, and nearly as amazing to me is that I found my way back to the base just as Danny got airborne again. We joined up and completed an otherwise uneventful first combat sortie. After we landed, the supervisor of flying, a hardened former Navy test pilot, looked up from his desk as I approached and with more a snarl than a smile said, "Pressure makes diamonds."

Combat experiences are often the luck of the draw. For some pilots, they take to the skies, and all is quiet and peaceful. My deployment was the opposite, and returning home I had experienced more kinetic employments (the use of weapons) than anyone in my squadron. Because I was the most junior aviator of the squadron, my commanders thought it best that my additional duties be limited so that I wouldn't feel overwhelmed. But free time after flying an intense combat mission didn't really feel like down time, so I volunteered most of mine at the Balad Theater Hospital. At that time the hospital had a 98 percent survival rate, which was astounding after seeing what an improvised explosive device (IED) can do to a human body. Working at the hospital, most particularly the helicopter pad and emergency room, was the most meaningful thing I've ever done. I have no medical training and rarely was involved with more than manual labor such as retrieving gurneys from the helicopter and transporting the injured to the ER. But I was able to talk to some of the soldiers, attempted to comfort some of the locals who were brought in, and saw the war up close and personal as compared to the bird's-eye view of the F-16.

Arriving back in New Mexico was surreal. It was the holidays, and everyone was in a celebratory mood. It was hard to square that with what I knew was happening on the other side of the globe. Traditionally the first combat squadron a pilot serves in will provide a fighter pilot with a call sign that is based on some sort of mistake by the pilot or a descriptor of that pilot's personality. There had been so little time between my arrival at the squadron and our deployment that mine wasn't given until we got back. After much late-night debate from the raucous group of thirty or so pilots in the squadron, I walked away forevermore known as "Glick." The name pays homage to my heritage as a Jew and reminds me every time I hear it just how much a role providence has played in my life. *Glick* is the Yiddish word for luck.

My life has been blessed by opportunity and the caring of others. The letters Norm sent me weekly for a year are just among the thousands of critical interactions he and I have had. I'm certain that I would not have pursued my dreams had Norm not been there to encourage me, and I likely would not have found the grit and determination I have today without his ability to reach me. The history he related wouldn't motivate everybody, but rather what makes the year of his letters so special is that Norm saw what would inspire me and brought those stories to me when I most needed them. My experiences in the Air Force—from the day I was sworn in through the present, having exchanged my flight suit again for a suit and tie—have guided

Daytime visor.

much of my life and the way I wish to live it. The lessons I've taken are often the simplest. How to focus, compartmentalize, and multitask. When to speak and when to listen. Striving for continual improvement and embracing change even in chaos. Most of all, it's about people: those you serve beside and those you serve, the people you love and those who love you. Norm certainly has embodied all these values throughout my life and will forever be someone I love and feel so lucky to have as a bona fide inspiration.

Epilogue

"Birth is a beginning and death a destination. And life is a journey."

—Jewish reading

IT IS SAID THAT 80 PERCENT OF SUCCESS IN life is just showing up. Greg always showed up. While others have fallen by the wayside over the years, Greg has remained steadfast in support of my many harebrained schemes, including a failed invention and long-shot writing projects. I can think of no one else who has come close to staying so positive and optimistic over many years. This has always been a bright spot in our relationship. He was never patronizing or enabling of folly, but rather his affirmation was the real deal.

Nothing has changed. We still communicate regularly about both the hard and soft subjects. At my advanced age it is still good to know that my importance to him has not diminished in the slightest. I can't imagine that it ever will.

Much has happened in the past decade or so since this journey began. Gen. Breedlove died a peaceful death on January 9, 2016, and was buried with honors at his birthplace in Franklin, Kentucky, next to his beloved wife, Mary Ann. A few days earlier, his funeral in Lubbock, Texas, included a thrilling low-level flyover of an airplane sent from Cannon Air Force Base near Clovis, New Mexico. Both Greg and Ryan were in attendance.

Opal Keith, my beloved mother-in-law, died peacefully on September 18, 2021. As long as she was able, she responded to requests to speak to religious and civic groups about her unique experience as one of the first WAVES in World War II.

Gen. Newman is now ninety-eight and remains active with his Jewish community in Oklahoma City. He generously has helped with development of this book by providing supplementary anecdotal information as well as editorial assistance.

After recovering from surgery and declared cancer-free, I returned to a full-time career as a psychologist in Lubbock. One of my specialties is trauma intervention, particularly with combat vets who suffer from PTSD. I am thankful to have been given the opportunity to continue to be of service to my community and patients and to be able to complete this project.

In 2008, upon learning that his beloved Tacos would be losing all twenty of their F-16s to the Washington, DC, National Guard unit, Greg resigned from the Air Force and returned to civilian life. He was not about to fly cargo planes. He joined the Air Force to become a combat fighter pilot. He became one, he did what he was trained to do, and he would leave the service as a fighter pilot. An ironic twist to this decision occurred on April 4, 2017, when the F-16 (number 306) in which he "cleared his rails"—that is, successfully delivered his bomb load—caught fire and was destroyed after its pilot bailed out. A model of that exact aircraft sits on my desk at work to this day, a constant reminder of Greg's accomplishments and what could have happened.

Another interesting sidebar to this story occurred during the summer of 2018. A man who looked vaguely familiar approached my wife and me in a restaurant. He introduced himself as Col. Roger Cude, whose wife I treated while she was battling cancer over twenty-five years earlier. Recognizing his service as an instructor pilot at the time as something from which Greg might benefit (which Col. Cude still performs to this day in a NATO capacity), I asked the colonel if he would mind giving Greg a tour of Reese AFB in Lubbock.

Not only did we get a thorough tour, Col. Cude arranged for Greg to have his first cockpit simulator ride, which beats any videogame then or since. This experience was one of the early building blocks of Greg's initial interest in flight, something I will always be grateful to Col. Cude for graciously reinforcing. The reward for the colonel was that he learned that one of his "students" made it to the top echelon of the fighter-jet world.

Greg returned to civilian life and resumed his career as president and chairman of Las Vegas Bancorp. He has been busy growing the bank while parenting two really good kids, Abby, now thirteen, and Sam, twelve. After nine years of marriage, he divorced in 2014.

I conclude with a brief elaboration on an anecdote mentioned previously about Greg's call sign. As explained, pilots name each other in the manner that best characterizes them. Sometimes these names are given in jest, other times as compliments. Occasionally, they are simply descriptive. Greg's call sign was all of the above and historical as well. Partially as a tribute to his Jewishness and to the greatest Jewish fighter pilot of all time, Flt. Lt. Robert Stanford Tuck, he was assigned the call sign "Glick," which means "lucky" in Yiddish. "Lucky" was Tuck's call sign as well. (Ironically, I have had a great friend, Neil Glickstein, whom I have called "Glick" since elementary school.) History had come full circle.

References

Publications, Manuscripts, and Oral Histories

Bendersky, Joseph W. *The Jewish Threat*. New York: Basic Books, 2000.

Breedlove, James. Audiovisual history as told to Mindy Rice, 1999. Transcript in Mindy Rice's possession.

Brown, Don, and Jerry Yellin. *The Last Fighter Pilot*. Washington, DC: Regnery, 2017.

Cohen, Rich. *The Avengers*. New York: Knopf, 2000.

Cummins, Keith. *Cataclysm: The War on the Eastern Front*. Solihull: Helion and Co., 2011.

Dapin, Mark. *Jewish Anzacs*. Sydney: NewSouth Books, 2017.

Dinnerstein, Leonard. *Anti-Semitism in America*. New York: Oxford University Press, 1994.

Forrester, Larry. *Fly for Your Life*. London: Cerberus, 2002.

Gilbert, Martin. *The Illustrated Atlas of Jewish Civilization*. New York: Macmillan, 1990.

Gitelman, Zvi. "Why They Fought: What Soviet Jewish Soldiers Saw and How It Is Remembered." NCEER Working Paper. Seattle: University of Washington Press, 2011.

Harrison, Donald H. "Did Anti-Semitism Block Medals for Rocker's Namesake?" *San Diego Jewish Press-Heritage*, April 13, 2001.

Henderson, Bruce. *Sons and Soldiers*. New York: HarperCollins, 2017.

Jacobs, Jerry. Unpublished memoirs. 1998. In author's possession.

Kershaw, Alex. *The Few.* New York: Da Capo, 2006.

Leibson, Art. *Sam Dreben: The Fighting Jew.* Tucson, AZ: Westerlore, 1996.

Levenson, Sam. Oral history as told to Greg Levenson, 1998. In Greg Levenson's possession.

Mosesson, Gloria R. *The Jewish War Veterans Story.* Washington, DC: Jewish War Veterans of the United States of America, 1971.

Penslar, Derek J. *Jews and the Military: A History.* Princeton, NJ: Princeton University Press, 2013.

Shulman, Norman M. "Completing the Circle: A Return to the Roots in Bialystok." *Reconstructionist Journal* 45, no. 1 (1979): 12–19, 29.

———. "My Son, the Fighter Pilot." *Jewish Veteran* 61, no. 1 (2008): 10–11.

———. "Myths of the Jewish Soldier and Athlete." *Jewish Outlook* 38, no. 3 (2002): A30–A31.

Tuck, Robert S. Flight log, 1940–1945. In Greg Levenson's possession.

Wolk, Bruce H. *Jewish Aviators in World War II.* Jefferson, NC: McFarland and Company, 2016.

Zubrin, Robert. "Rickover and the Nuclear Navy." *Furion* 7, no. 4 (July–August 1985): 8–16.

Websites

Information on ancestry, immigration, the US armed forces, and US military history is available at many authoritative websites. The following sites were particularly useful in researching Jews in the Air Force and the US military in general, as well as the State of Israel's military history.

References

Jewish Agency for Israel: https://www.jewishagency.org/
Jewish Magazine: https://jewishmag.com
Jewish Virtual Library: Jewishvirtuallibrary.org
Jewish War Veterans of the United States of America:
        https://www.jwv.org/
Jewish World Review: https://jewishworldreview.com
San Diego Jewish World: http://www.sdjewishworld.com

Index

Krigelman, Robert, *121*

Levenson, Sam, 10, 105
Levitow, John, 64, 66
Levy, Simon M., 91
Levy, Uriah P., 91
Litvyak, Lydia, 85, 175–76
Luke Air Force Base, 197, 210

Maccabee, Judah the, 9, 52, 73
Mamedoff, Andrew B. ("Mad
  Russian"), 77–78
Marcus, Mickey, 27–28
Margolis, Irv, *109*
Margolis, Milton, *109*
Marix, Adolph, 81
McAuliffe, Christa, 37, 196
Medal of Honor, 10, 46, 58, 61,
  101, 102
Moody Air Force Base, 194,
  209
Mordecai, Alfred, 81

Nelson, William ("Wild Bill"),
  93–94
Newman, Stan, 69–71, *70, 71*,
  222

Operation Iraqi Freedom, 212

Pale of Settlement, 160, 189
Peck, Gregory, 4, 60–61
Pershing, John J., 150, 152

Proskauer, Adolph, 43
post-traumatic stress disorder
  (PTSD), 35, 201, 222
Pyramid of Jewish Heroes, *9*

Reese Air Force Base, 205, 223
Rickover, Hyman, 58
Royal Air Force (RAF), 71–73
Rubin, Tibor, 97–98

Salomon, Edward, 156
Salomon, Hayman, 165–66
Salonika, Greece, 17, 18
Salvador, Francis, 89–90
Sawelson, William, 62
Schlamberg, Philip, 202–3
Segal, Harold, 116–18
Shiver, Helene, 158–59
Slanger, Frances, 85
Smith, Goldwin, 8
Sommer, George, 32
Spector, Iftach, 128

Tolkowsky, Dan, 129
Torres, Albert, 17
Tuck, Robert S., 10, 73–76, 157,
  223
Twain, Mark, 8, 114

Undergraduate Pilot Training
  (UPT), 5, 166

van Mentz, Brian, 75, 94